Traveling
Deliberately

MINIMIZING STRESS AND
MAXIMIZING FULFILLMENT
DURING YOUR JOURNEY

STEVE BANNOW

ARCHWAY
PUBLISHING

Archway Publishing books may be ordered through booksellers or by contacting:

Archway Publishing
1663 Liberty Drive
Bloomington, IN 47403
www.archwaypublishing.com
1-(888)-242-5904

ISBN: 978-1-4808-1040-2 (sc)
ISBN: 978-1-4808-1041-9 (e)

Library of Congress Control Number: 2014950331

Printed in the United States of America.

Archway Publishing rev. date: 9/18/2014

"I went to the woods because I wished to live deliberately, to front only the essential facts of life, and see if I could not learn what it had to teach, and not, when I came to die, discover that I had not lived."

Henry David Thoreau
From *Walden; or, Life in the Woods*

Acknowledgements

To: Barbara, Aenea, Andrew, Bounkhain, Braham, Charles, Chris, Deb, Debbie, Di, Elissa, Gilda, Harry, Jack, Jeannette, Josh, Karen, Kay, Kit, Margarita, Mark, Maryann, Mehtap, Mike, Pete, Ricky, Rob, Santiago, Stacy, Stewart, Sue, Susan, Tang, and Wachinton.

My sincere thanks to each of you for having a hand in this project.

With Love,

S

Preface

This book represents the collective advice and wisdom that I have gained from some very bright folks, many of whom have quite literally been all over the world, as well as from a fair amount of reading and research and plenty of on-the-road experience.

For those of you who are contemplating significant international travel for the first time, dive in! There is much to discover and plan for, and there is a lot of fun to be had in doing so. Those of you who have already been around a bit will have given some time and attention to a number of the subjects that I address in my book. I would bet, however, that taking the opportunity to have a close look at what I have to say will also serve *you* well as you plan and then take your next trip.

In any case, for just about everyone the greatest challenge of long-term, multi-country travel is having some idea of how to create a general plan that prevents problems from occurring in the first place and how to live a regimen that will keep major hassles, stress, and unwelcome spikes in blood pressure to a minimum. Believe me, long-term, multi-country travel is about as good as life can be, but it is not as easy as it looks.

Give me a chance in these pages to help you get the most out of your journey.

Contents

Introduction

First, let's be clear about what this book is *not*. What you are about to read is not quite a few things. It is not a guide to the finest museums of Europe, the most compelling antiquities of Asia, the most captivating wildlife viewing in Africa, the finest beaches in Australia, the greatest restaurants in the Americas, or the most spectacular views in Antarctica. These things I leave for you to research on your own or discuss with your travel agent, or (better yet) both. (And then you can have a good look in person and decide for yourself!) No, this book is not about *what* to see. The focus of this book is on *how* to prepare for and then go about seeing it. My purpose is to help make long-term travel as crisis-free and uncomplicated as possible—to keep your anxiety and stress level down and your spirits and fulfillment level up.

While we're at it, let's clarify something else: my intended audience. While I think anyone planning virtually any international trip can benefit by spending some time with this small book, my real target readers are adults—not necessarily Americans—on an extended holiday who plan to be away from home for at least a month and to visit more than one or a handful of countries during their travels. The type of travel that I am addressing in these pages is, frankly, challenging and complicated. It should certainly not be feared, but long-term, multi-country travel must be approached with thoughtful consideration and respect. I am hopeful that what I have learned through research, observations, and my own experience (including my share of mistakes) will lessen your physical and, especially, your emotional load and help you to get as much as possible from your journey. After all, what experience (other than having a family and possibly work) can offer more fulfillment than the perspective-enlarging, jaw-dropping, life-altering wonders of travel?

Now, I think it's only fair to tell you a bit about me. This should help with important things like perspective, motive, and purpose. As I write this, I am a sixty-two year old, physically fit (except for two screaming knees), arthritic (neck, shoulders, lower back, knees, and wrists) nonsmoker. I have a solid retirement from the US Navy after over twenty-four years of service as a JAG. I receive a monthly VA check, I have a small retirement income from the State of Florida, and I decided to draw social security as soon as I could—starting last June. I am certainly not rich, but my point in mentioning my finances is to be upfront about what can be done without being a millionaire. If you are a millionaire, congratulations! I am going to assume, however, that wasting money is stressful for all of us no matter what our financial situations may be and should be avoided.

Extensive travel has not been a life-long ambition for me. I certainly had my share of international travel during my years with the navy, but it did not become a passion until just a few years ago—before my first visit to New Zealand, Australia, and Southeast Asia. I have found that three things are very important, if not vital, for those of us who wish to travel over an extended period of time to a variety of countries:

good health, few significant ties to the home front, and *financial independence.* These things are all relative, of course, but they are all applicable in my case. Although I have significant issues with arthritis (which I deal with by staying in motion, plenty of glucosamine and MSM supplements, and meditative channeling), my health and fitness are excellent. I no longer run, but I can walk all day. I am single but blessed with having a loving, patient woman in my life. I have no children, but I do have a terrific sister and several nieces and nephews, as well as grandnieces and grandnephews, who love me but do not *need* me. Oh yes, I sold my house and my car and either sold or gave away just about all of my other stuff. This was liberating, I assure you. And, for now, I am on a hiatus from work.

Additionally, I think it is well to note that while I have certainly been around, you probably know people who have been to more countries than I have. Not many folks have had the opportunity, however, to stay on the road for as long as I did during my last trip. (Please take a look at my list of countries visited in Appendix I.) I think the key to understanding this list—especially considering my purpose and my audience—is *how* I planned for and then actually went about my travels during my last journey. For several important reasons that I hope will make sense in the pages that follow, the places I planned to visit and ultimately did visit were grouped together geographically for periods that ranged from a few weeks to several months in duration.

I will also offer a word here about the structure of this book. I have worked hard to be succinct without being simplistic or glib. This approach is inherent in the number and length of the chapters—each making and quickly explicating an important point. A few of these points/chapters require a little extra attention and are either broken down into subsections or given greater depth by my use of footnotes and appendices.

Finally, I don't profess to have all of the answers. Talk to others, including your travel agent, friends, and family members who have been around. Do some research, read, and get involved. If you do your homework, I think that you will find the consciousness-raising that I attempt in these pages will help you—in some cases, a great deal. And I can promise that keeping your anxiety and stress down and enthusiasm and spirits up will make a huge difference. Moreover, I want this to be the book that I wish I had read prior to October 2010—before my first extensive travel. As I noted earlier, even if you have been around, this little book should be worth a look. While I like to think that virtually everything in these pages has some relevance if not importance to your travels, some things are especially important. To avoid unnecessary discussion, I have attempted to highlight the absolute essentials. The chapter titles are the keys. If you ignore my suggestions and advice on these items, you might as well not read the book at all. These points are at the very heart of traveling *deliberately* and increasing the odds against a ruined day or week or trip or even jeopardizing your health instead of enjoying a truly fulfilling, low-hassle journey.

Now let's get started.

Chapter 1

Getting Started

Whoa! Hold your horses! You aren't going anywhere yet. The first thing and, in many ways the single most important thing, is the *plan*. Give yourself plenty of time to develop an itinerary that makes sense for you and your objectives while factoring in seasonal considerations, allowing ample time to take advantage of good deals for early booking, and doing everything else your research has taught you.

Here are some key questions that you need to answer:

1. How long do you have to travel?

2. Where would you like to go? (Be sure to prioritize your list.)

3. What do you want to do?
   ecotourism
   physical challenge

touring from a train/bus
cultural
city or rural emphasis or both
animal observation
some combination or all of the above

4. What type of accommodations do you want?
   1-5 stars
   backpackers/hostels
   camping
   some combination or all of the above

Now, to help yourself answer these questions, you should consider your own previous travel experiences, independent research (including some important and very helpful reading—please see Appendix III), conversations with friends and family, and a recommended travel agent. My travel *plan* stage included all of these resources, but the linchpin was and still is my travel agent.[1]

Once the basic questions about your itinerary have been answered, assemble your trip plan. Here's how I went about it for my latest journey. First, I created a wish list of the countries that I wanted to visit. Second, I prioritized the countries

---

[1] Okay ... okay, time for full disclosure. My agent's name is Mark Gerling of Gerling Travel, Flagler Beach, Florida. You are going to have to trust me on this. At this writing, he has no idea I am even mentioning him or his company in my book. If he offered to compensate me for the reference, I would not accept it. This book is for *you,* and I want you to have the best trip possible. So give Mark a call or not, but please consider carefully having the helpful, steady hand of an experienced and competent travel agent to help with planning and issues along the way. I have relied on Mark more than a few times, and the success of my mostly stress-free, life-altering travels has been in every sense of the word, a *team* effort.

on my list, removing those that were too remote vis-à-vis the others on my list, those that were too dangerous, and those that could wait until next time. Third, keeping in mind the seasons, I placed the countries in a weather-wise geographical order. Fourth, I consciously chose to begin my journey in places where travel and living were relatively easy to handle and then working up to more challenging locales. Finally, I shared the plan with my travel agent who served as listener, supporter, devil's advocate, and partner. (As one who is primarily a solo traveler, I have found that my travel agent has been especially significant to me. Throughout this guide I will be providing examples of the importance of having a first-rate travel agent watching your back—at least from a distance—whether you are traveling alone or not. My travel agent's help was hugely travel-enhancing and much more.)

And here is what *we* ended up with:

2013	*End of January*	Hawaii (return to visit friends)
	February	New Zealand (return to visit friends)
	March	Australia (return to visit friends)
	Early April	Singapore (transit)
	April	South Africa (focus on Cape Town)
		Madagascar (sightseeing, animal observation, hiking)
		Return to South Africa (the bush and wildlife)
		Zimbabwe (focus on Victoria Falls and wildlife)
		Zambia (focus on Zambezi River and wildlife)

	Mozambique (beach, ocean, personal battery-charging)
May	Malawi (focus on Lake Malawi)
	Tanzania (the bush and wildlife)
	Kenya (brief return trip and transit)
	Ethiopia (primarily transit)
	Egypt (Cairo, Giza, antiquities, the Nile)
	Dubai (visit friends, sightseeing, personal battery-charging)
	Maldives (island life, the ocean, the beach, snorkeling)
June	Turkey (Istanbul, antiquities, sightseeing, hiking, hot-air ballooning)
	Greece (Athens, antiquities, multi-island cruise, hiking, sightseeing)
	Cyprus (sightseeing)
	Hungary, Serbia, Croatia, Bulgaria, Romania, Danube River Cruise[2]
	Austria (Vienna, Innsbruck, hiking, sightseeing)
	Switzerland (Zurich, Bern, Wengen, hiking, sightseeing)
July	Italy (sightseeing, hiking, antiquities, multi-city—most travel by train)

---

[2] Mark and I discussed at considerable length my desire to visit this part of Europe and the best options for doing so. We chose a ten-day Viking cruise on the Danube from Budapest to Bucharest. Heavy spring rains caused the river to rise considerably and significantly changed the game plan. I will have much more to say in chapter 16 about this part of the trip and how a balanced approach to travel turned this into one of my journey's highlights.

	Malta (quick three-day visit to Malta for sightseeing and hiking)
August	Canada (cross-country train trip with time for sightseeing, hiking, and fishing with stops in Jasper, Banff, and Vancouver among other places; also Yellowknife, Blachford Lake, and Whitehorse via light aircraft)
Early September	Alaska cruise
Mid-September–October	Michigan (break for visits to doctor and dentist and other personal business, time with loved ones and enjoying autumn colors in Michigan, as well as a brief trip to New England, New Brunswick, and Prince Edward Island)
November 2013–March 2014	South America segment with Buenos Aires apartment as home base
November 7–15	Peru (Cusco, hiking Inca Trail, touring Machu Picchu)
November 16–20	Chile (exploring Rapa Nui/Easter Island)
December 1–11	Antarctica (cruise from Ushuaia to the Continent for exploring, mountain-climbing, snowshoeing, kayaking, animal observation)
December 25, 2013–January 1, 2014	Ecuador (Galapagos Islands for sightseeing, hiking, snorkeling, animal observation, cycling)

January 12–15	Iguazú Falls, Argentina (exploring, sightseeing, hiking)
January 16–18	Paraguay (focus on Asunción)
February 1–14	Buenos Aires and Montevideo, Uruguay while friends from US visited
February 17–25	Chile (Patagonia white-water rafting and kayaking on Futaleufú River[3])
February 28	Hasta Luego to Buenos Aires
March 1–13	Bolivia (focus on sightseeing and exploring Lake Titicaca)
	Colombia (focus on touring Bogotá)
	Venezuela (planned excursion to Angel Falls canceled due to injury; brief stay in Caracas limited by domestic turmoil)
	Dominican Republic (personal battery-charging at a hotel)
	Bahamas (Rendezvous with Barbara at an island resort)

Yes, I know. This was an ambitious trip—a trip of a lifetime in fact. What is so incredible is that it was even better as a wonder-filled, life-altering *experience.* There were certainly some times of stress, some close calls, and even some health issues. Excellent planning, a willingness to stick with the basics

---

[3] Injury—A freak accident that resulted in a broken rib and other injuries on my second day of rafting totally disrupted any further activity during my stay at the Bio/Bio camp on the river. Please see my discussion of travel insurance in chapter 20 to learn how my carrier (Travelex) responded to my claim for trip interruption.

discussed in this book, and the occasional timely assistance and intervention of my travel agent, however, kept the anxieties low and the joys and rewards of travel sky high. By the way, purchasing travel insurance, which covered most of my journey, brought me great peace of mind. Cancellations, injuries in extremely remote areas, and even death are always possible during long-term, multi-country travel. Insurance is one good way to manage those risks. Please strongly consider purchasing insurance during your planning stage. It is expensive, but it is a very wise hedge against disaster. I have more to say about this in chapter 20.

In closing this chapter, I want to offer a brief review of the itinerary-planning by taking a quick look back at the sequence and timing of my multi-country, year-plus journey. Note how I started out easy, first in the United States with English-speaking Hawaii during a great time of year to escape winter (late January) and then on to two other English-speaking countries where I already had friends and the infra-structure is excellent. And, since I was south of the equator, their summer was cruising along. From there things started to get more complicated as I began a tricky multi-country/multi-lingual/multi-cultural trek through some challenging but incredible African countries. At this point, however, I was primed and ready for the additional dynamics.

Next came time for my European adventure. What better time to arrive for a two-week swing through Europe than late spring? The torrential spring rains and flooding that followed in central Europe became issues that had to be dealt with, but resilience and a change in plans kept the weather from doing little, if anything, to distract me. (More on this in chapter 16.)

Then it was back to North America for some wonderful travel time in Canada and Alaska—a treat to be sure and certainly not arduous by any means. After almost eight straight months on the road, it came time to regroup briefly (always a good option), for checking in with my doctor and dentist, and for taking a bit of a break. I worked this hiatus into my itinerary at the outset, and I am very glad that I did.

After I was fully seasoned as a long-term traveler with my batteries completely recharged, it was on to South America for four and a half more months of exploration while keeping a home base in Buenos Aires. I was certainly well prepared at this point to be totally immersed in a very different culture where language would be a constant issue[4] and eating, drinking, and all of the rest of life's basics would present challenges in Argentina and in the other countries (and one additional continent) that I visited during my South America adventure. Once again, the weather was excellent, as I arrived in the Argentinian springtime. In fact, the weather was quite welcoming in virtually every country I visited on the continent, and it was even relatively pleasant in Antarctica, where it was less cold at the time of my visit than it was in most of the Midwest United States.

With the essentials of your planning plan now established, you are ready to start putting it all together, setting dates, buying tickets, and all the other fun things to do as you set your sights on your embarkation date. Right? Well, not quite. There is still one huge question to consider *carefully*: your travel companion(s).

---

[4] I do speak some Spanish, but I am certainly not proficient with the language. I will have much more to say about the challenges of communication in chapter 12.

Chapter 2

Traveling Companions

For some of you, this chapter is unnecessary. For example, if you are married and have been planning your extended, multi-country dream journey for two for years, go ahead and grab your spouse, leave the children at home, and hit the road. The tougher choices concerning fellow travelers await those with children who for one reason or another can't be left behind, singletons who are apprehensive about making a long journey alone, and those who may find themselves in the middle of a group of would-be travelers.

I can't overemphasize how important it is to give this issue very serious consideration. Remember, your companion is a person who is going to be a virtual part of you for months at a time—through some of the best, some of the most challenging, and occasionally some of the most routine times in your life. It's like a roommate situation on steroids. So, the bottom line for success is long-term compatibility. In many ways long-term travel with a companion (or companions) is more intense than marriage.

I learned while on my first extended trip (from October 2010 to July 2011) that I do best on my own. I began with a travel companion, but I did not finish with one. Honestly, there was no one to blame; no one was at fault. My companion's responsibilities on the home front and different (not completely compatible) needs, habits, and view of life made the decision to go our separate ways not a difficult one. What I learned about travel during my extended first trip, my overall excellent mental and physical fitness, my confidence level, and my general self-reliance have made me—at least up to this point—my own best long-term travel companion. It is well to note here that occasionally my itinerary did call for me to link up with tour groups of various sizes. For the most part, these excursions went well, as I managed to find sufficient time to be on my own. My very best companions, however, were the first-rate, one-on-one guides, several of whom are now close friends, who helped to make so many segments of my travel truly "wonder full." In any case, you should always be diligent about finding someone whom you trust to have your back to at least some extent.

So for now let's focus on the person with the most obvious dilemma: someone who does not want to travel alone and has more than one friend or family member who would like to go along and has the means to do so.

You and your travel companion will be joined at the hip. Once again, *compatibility is vital*. Everything else on your trip can be well planned and in theory can be ideal, but if you are not happy with your companion you will go to sleep each night and wake up each morning stressed out and not having much fun. I could go on about this, but you get the message.

And here is my final point. Remember the old maxim from your grade school days: "Two's company; three's a crowd." This applies to most travel companion scenarios. First, people are dynamic. Even unselfish, considerate souls have their own priorities, idiosyncrasies, and objectives. Every time you add another person to the basic travel team, you increase the dynamics—and the possibility of some level of turmoil—exponentially.

If this isn't enough, keep in mind the challenges of odd numbers. At some point, alliances can form, and the odd person may be left out. This is not pleasant for *anyone*. I am aware that this may sound like fear-mongering with a slice of misanthropy thrown in. Not so. I genuinely like folks, and most would say I am really good at just getting along—without resenting it while I am doing so. I am just trying to keep unnecessary stressors out of the equation, especially at the planning stage, and I firmly believe that less is more; the notion of "the more the merrier" is not necessarily the answer. Ultimately, however, you know yourself (and your potential travel companions) best, and you will make the call. Just give this component plenty of consideration. If you do decide to travel with a partner or partners, by all means remember the civility lessons you were taught as a child and put them into play. Kindness, courtesy, patience, generosity, and consideration are so absolutely vital when living closely with others for long periods. Even if your partner has forgotten or never mastered these life skills, make certain they are second nature for you—*always*. The success of your trip and your partner's trip could depend on how *you* behave.

So, are we at the starting line yet? Well, not to put too fine an edge on it ... no. We are not yet ready to launch. We still need to discuss your endurance, your strength, and maybe your waistline.

Chapter 3

Fitness

No matter what your age—whether you are twenty or ninety—you are going to get much more out of your travels if your weight is under control and you are reasonably fit. If you have been living the life of a couch potato and you are feeling and looking like it, you need to turn things around *now* ... this minute!

You don't begin by bounding from the couch and doing twenty-five jumping jacks. You begin by making an appointment to see your doctor (and don't forget your dentist while you are paying attention to your health), for advice on a good, steady, *safe* fitness program. While you are awaiting your doctor and dentist appointments, start walking—a little at first and a little more each day. This really shouldn't be an issue for you unless your fitness has gone completely astray. And consider this: While you are out for your daily stroll, you can think about cool stuff like how great you are going to look and feel when you are back in shape and how much fun you are going to have on your trip as the new, healthy, fit you. By the way, *leave your iPod and anything else that requires earphones at home.* Get used to paying attention to things like where and how you are walking. Be alert; be in touch; listen for everything: your footsteps, your breathing, birds, dogs, and sirens. Use all of your senses when you walk; this is excellent training for moving about in totally new places. For your safety and increased pleasure, *pay attention when you walk*!

When you finally get in to see your doctor, tell her what you have in mind and where you intend to go *and* tell her that I said you need to be healthy and fit. She'll help you design a program that will help you shed some unnecessary pounds and increase your endurance for those planned and sometimes unplanned hikes. Your program should also emphasize increasing your physical strength. Resistance training is a good thing to do in any case, but it will also be a really good way to prepare for those times—often unplanned—when you have to schlepp your own bags when a transfer does not show up to take you to your next stop.

Your doctor visit is also the time to determine which vaccinations you will need and when you need to get them. Remember, some shots like the Hepatitis B series vaccination must be administered over time with breaks of up to a month or more in between. Also, be extra careful to check if malaria prophylaxis is needed or even recommended for the areas you wish to visit. If so, *get the pills and take them religiously.* If you are not going to do this, then stay home. I mean it! And bear in mind that not all malaria meds are the same. Be sure that yours are suitable for exactly where you are going. I used atovaquone-proguanil—good stuff for Tanzania and other places in southeast Africa, with minimal side effects. Just bear in mind that no antimalarial is one hundred percent effective. Augment your meds by being proactive in other ways. When in malaria regions, wear long-sleeved shirts and long pants, use mosquito netting around your bed, try to avoid sleeping in areas that have relatively high mosquito populations, and try to avoid outside activity at dawn and dusk.[5]

Your doctor visit is also the time to order the extra meds that you will need to take with you. You may also wish to talk about supplements to help you with fitness, alertness, and strength. I have done well with vitamin B complex, vitamin D, and magnesium, for example. Whether to take these supplements, others, or none at all is, of course, a decision that you must make with your doctor.

And I wasn't joking about seeing your dentist just before you leave on your trip. First of all, dental fitness is a fundamental component of overall good health. Also, bear in mind that many great journeys have been interrupted or ruined because of dental problems. You can't assure that your travel will be one hundred percent free of dental issues, but you can certainly dramatically increase the odds by implementing excellent preventive dental care. I'll have more to say about dental hygiene and care later, but for now, *make that dental appointment!*

---

[5] Be sure to have a look at the Centers for Disease Control and Prevention (CDC) Yellow Book for many more health care tips.

Chapter 4

Travel Documents

Another key component of your trip preparations is securing all of the necessary travel documents. This may be another one of my painfully obvious points, but what may not be quite so obvious is *what* exactly you need and *when* you need to start the process of acquisition.

You should start with your passport. You aren't going anywhere—not even Canada—without one (or an equivalent). If you do not already have your passport, start the process *now*. If you do have a passport but it will expire during your journey or even within six months of your planned return home, start the process for renewal *now*.[6] Obtaining

---

[6] Some countries require that a passport be valid for at least six months beyond the end of your visit. In fact, some airlines will not even let you board if this requirement is not met. For much more on this and related passport issues, including the costs of different types of passport books and cards, consult the US Department of State, Bureau of Consular Affairs, link at travel.state. gov/content/English/passports/FAQs.html. I also have more to say on this topic in the following paragraphs.

a new passport is not a particularly difficult task, but it can take time—normally from four to six weeks from the date the application is submitted. You can go for expedited service which takes half the time, but this will cost an extra $60, and part of my job in keeping your stress and disappointment in check is to help you avoid spending money needlessly. So start the process *now* and keep the $60 for expedited service in your pocket.

In some cases (Brazil and Vietnam, for example), you will need a special visa that cannot be obtained in the normal fashion at an airport upon arrival. Not all countries require visas for travelers from the United States, but some do, and the process can be a pain and may require that you already have a passport to begin with. Let's talk about Brazil for a moment. This will serve as a good example of the more rigorous visa acquisition processes. For travel to and in this spectacular country, you must obtain a Brazilian visa *in advance* from the Brazilian embassy or a consulate nearest to your place of residence in the United States. My advice is to consider a call to the main Brazilian consulate at (202)461-3000. (This number was good as of April 2014.) There are also consulates in Atlanta, Boston, Chicago, Hartford, Houston, Las Angeles, Miami, New York City, and San Francisco. Better yet, have a look at the Brazilian embassy website for additional relevant information. The processing time for the visa can take between ten and fourteen days. I should note here that a few countries (Australia and Sri Lanka, for example) now require Electronic Travel Authority (ETA) in addition to a valid passport for entry. This is very easy to do on line *before* you enter the country. I expect to see more countries using this procedure in the future.

While it is possible to obtain your visa by using a visa service or visa agency, this will require you to give up your passport for two weeks or more. I *hate* not having my passport in my possession, so I very rarely part with it. Additionally, for arranging travel to Brazil or other countries that have special or advance visa requirements—especially when you are already on the road—this and virtually *any* passport-related issue can be resolved at the US embassy.[7] Having to do this, however, is time-consuming and, yes, stressful. Your best bet is to take the time to go to the consulate well in advance of your departure. And, by the way, this entire process can be made much simpler and far less stressful if you *work closely with your travel agent during the early planning stage of your travel preparations.*

Yet another passport-related concern is the number of blank pages that you have available in your current passport even if it will not expire for years. Upon the advice of my travel agent and based on information found at travel.state.gov, I sent mine to the National Passport Processing Center (Post Office Box 90106, Philadelphia, PA 19190-0106 for routine requests and Post Office Box 90906 zip code 19190-0906 for expedited requests) with an application (Form DS-4085) requesting extra pages. In about two weeks I received my passport with additional pages A through X inserted. Once again, thanks to some good planning, I had no concerns about running out of space for visas and stamps. Yes, I know, I know … I had to relinquish control of my passport for a while, but it really needed to be done. The process is not complicated, and the entire transaction took place in the United States with plenty of time to spare.

---

[7]   A partial list of such countries that may be of interest to you would include China, Vietnam, Bhutan, Russia, Belarus, and India.

If you plan to include Argentina in your journey, you have more work to do: you must submit your form and payment for your reciprocity fee (currently $160 for Americans, $100 for Australians, and $70 for Canadians). While fairly reliable reports indicate that the requirement is currently being enforced only at Ezeiza International Airport in Buenos Aires, this is one time when I am advocating for the expenditure of funds. Consider it a cost of doing business in order to have fun in a really cool country. Once you pay your fee, you will receive a document on line that you must print and carry with you. In fact, you may be asked to present it fairly frequently, so keep it handy. Other South American countries such as Chile, Brazil, Bolivia, and Paraguay require similar entrance fees or visas, but Argentina is the most rigid in its requirement of payment and documentation before you even *board* your international Buenos Aires-bound plane.

Depending on your specific travel plans, you may have additional documentation requirements. Perhaps the most important of these is your official yellow-fever card, which provides proof of your yellow-fever vaccination. Obviously, it is a shot that could save your life, but it is the card that will save you serious hassles when you attempt to enter certain African and South American countries. By the way, your best resource for information regarding vaccinations that are recommended or, more important, *required* is the Centers for Disease Control and Prevention (CDC) website. And once again, your travel agent and your doctor are essential assets in helping you to make the correct decisions regarding vaccinations and prophylactic medications. You should also bring copies of doctor's orders for all of your prescription meds. Some countries require such documentation upon entry, but it also can be very helpful if you need a refill while you are on the road.

Carrying copies of the first (main) page of your passport, additional passport-sized photos, and a certified *copy* (not the original) of your birth certificate can prove to be helpful. These items take up very little space, and in my case they serve to foster my sense of wellbeing and deliberate traveling.

The great news about all of these documentation requirements is that, while they may take time and some cash to obtain, they are easy to carry and can be organized among your most important travel items in a logical and easy-to-use fashion. As is the case with at least a week's supply of your medications, your cash, and your passport, your key travel documents should always remain in your carry-on bags while you are actually traveling. *Never* place these items in your checked bags. I'll have more to say about this later, especially when I discuss packing in chapter 5.

In any discussion of what to include in a list (in this case, important travel documents), there is often a desire—at least on my part—to mention some items that one should leave at home. I am going to avoid listing the thousands of obvious things that have no business in your baggage and mention only three documents that you should *not* bring with you. I suppose there could be a need for one or all of these while you are away, but that need would be remote at best, and taking these items means more things to keep track of and more things that could be lost or stolen. So here is my super brief list of documents to leave at home: your original birth certificate, your original social security card, and (for those of you who have one) your military identification card. I have just a few additional words to say about the last of these. As you know, I am a retired naval officer. This means I possess an ID card that includes my name, branch of service, status (retired), rank, and so on. This is a handy item to have and use while in the United States. I am proud of it. Unfortunately, however, carrying a piece of ID that links me directly to the US armed services could prove complicated and even deadly in an extreme situation. It has no reasonable usefulness and could get lost or could get me into trouble. I leave it at home when I travel abroad and strongly encourage those of you who have one to do the same. Now let's get back to what you *do* need to take with you.

Chapter 5

Packing—Less Is More

In outlining this book, I was tempted to simply mention the checklists found at Appendix II at this point and then move on to the next topic, but upon further consideration I concluded that some discussion here could be of some help to you. So let's talk about what to pack ... and what *not* to.

You have heard it before. Pack lightly—especially clothing. The last thing you want to do is lug around unnecessary stuff that may require extra bags which will, in turn, cost you more. You are not traveling to another planet ... *yet*. You will find places to wash clothes, and no matter what the destination, there are plenty of places where you can buy items that you really do need. Buying locally means at least three things. You are getting what you need when you need it, you are acquiring automatic souvenirs, and you are helping the local economy. As for exactly what clothes you should take, the climate, the type of travel (e.g., adventure, cultural, low-impact sightseeing, or a combination of these), and the duration of your trip will all play a part. Simply applying some common sense, along with consulting with and carefully considering the advice of your travel agent and fellow travelers, will keep you on track. I like to go with the two Cs and a V: casual, comfortable, and versatile. In other words, pack clothes that are easy to wear and good for almost any kind of activity. By the way, although it is quite a stretch to consider ear plugs to be clothes, so be it. This is as good a place as any to give them special attention. Pack lots of these. You'll need them!

There is another piece of advice that you may have received about packing clothes: Roll, don't fold. Take that advice. Rolling actually does save room, and it also creates fewer wrinkles. And this is the point where I need to urge you to get away from your luggage (i.e., suitcases) no matter how chic or handy it may seem and get into a backpack. Backpacks are easily carried on your back where you are strongest, and they are relatively lightweight. This matters a lot when every extra pound could mean extra costs at check-in time, and it will make a huge difference when you have to walk several kilometers over uneven roads after you have missed your transport. Rolled clothes and backpacks are an excellent combo.

If you are traveling with a companion, interchange the items in your checked bags. The idea here is redundancy. If one traveler's bag is lost or damaged, the other traveler will have the necessities you each will need—at least for a while. And let me repeat an important caveat: Never pack really important stuff (e.g., travel documents, medications, money, or other valuables) in your checked bags. Be certain that your checked bag (your backpack) is easily recognizable and distinguishable—to you and others—and has helpful, legible identification information that will make it easy to get back to you if you become separated. For long-term, multi-country travel, lost baggage is almost inevitable. You will live through it. The key is to keep the anxiety and stress levels low when this nasty little nuisance does arise.

Oh yes, this is the time for me to provide a comment about umbrellas. As my Auntie used to say: "It's all fun and games until someone loses an eye!" Some checklists will urge you to pack a small one. My checklist does no such thing. You see, I *detest* umbrellas. They are awkward—no matter how compact—and they do nothing that a good set of rain gear can't do. Additionally, someone, usually someone much larger and less friendly than you are, inevitably gets poked or jabbed—even by you, the most considerate of all umbrella users. Also, with one unexpected good hard gust of wind, your umbrella will become just like millions before: broken and even more useless than it was previously. Please … no umbrellas.

Finally, I have a thought or two on adaptors and converters. You will almost certainly have to give some of your electronic gear an occasional charge or have the need to plug in something like a hair dryer. Your gear's plugs will often not match the sockets where you are staying. You have options here. You can buy and pack a "universal" adaptor/converter before you begin your journey; be advised that even really good "universals" usually aren't what their name implies. Or you can buy several that *should* match up with the various sockets that you will encounter while you are traveling. This, of course, involves bringing along more stuff with no guarantee that you will always be able to hook up. Or you can buy one locally to suit virtually any situation. These devices are usually only the equivalent of one or two bucks, and some local shopkeeper gets to make a sale, albeit a small one. I ended up embracing the third option.

It is now time for you to have a look at the packing checklist located at Appendix II. The contents of this checklist are, of course, only my suggestions. Feel free to tweak them according to your legitimate needs and in accordance with the advice of your travel agent and fellow travelers. Just remember: Less really is more.

Chapter 6

Staying Healthy

Y ou have heard it before. Nothing is more important than your health. Believe it. This is especially the case when you are away from home, loved ones, your personal health care providers, easy access to meds, and your own bed. So the key is to start your trip fit and healthy and to *stay* that way.

We have already discussed the need for you to set up a fitness program with your doctor well in advance of your travel date, and I have related the importance of having thorough checkups by your doctor and your dentist as well as the *absolute necessity* of obtaining all of the necessary vaccinations. And of course there is also the need to be certain that you have an adequate supply of your medications and the means to obtain more if necessary.

If you are fortunate enough to be in generally good health, my advice is simple: stay the course and keep moving. Even when you are nowhere near a gym, you can walk, schlepp your own bags, take the stairs, and do pushups, crunches, and jumping jacks. And, if you take supplements (e.g., CoQ10, fish oil, vitamin B, etc.), do your best to continue with them even though they can take up a fair amount of space in your backpack.

If your health requires a more sedentary life style, don't worry. If you are well enough to travel, you can certainly maintain some level of physical conditioning by finding reasonable exercise where and when you can. I'm still advocating for movement here: walking when you can walk and taking the stairs when you have an opportunity to do so. If walking is not possible, lift things. The bottom line here is that you have known yourself for a long time, and you know when you are slacking off from whatever exercise suits you, and you should also know when you have not been diligent about taking your health aids like medication and supplements. Listen to me: No letting up on your health just because you are on the road!

That brings me to the other part of the activity equation: rest and sleep. We've all known folks who seem to have boundless energy even with what appears to be very little sleep. I have no explanations for this phenomenon; I, too, stand in awe. Oh yes, another thing about these human dynamos is that many of them never seem to get sick … not even the sniffles. Good for them, but most of us are not wired that way. I, for example, am your Mod-1—the kind of guy who needs eight hours of sleep or more each night. I simply don't do or feel as well when I am cut short of my eight hours. And if I get substantially less than that for more than one day in a row, I do start running the risk of getting sick.

The reality is long-term, multi-country travel is eventually going to require occasional brutally early flight times—especially nasty if you are not a morning person. So be it. There are simple ways to fight back. One of these, for me at least, is *not* sleeping on the plane. I just can't seem to get any good sleep when I am flying. My solution is certainly not rocket science. I simply try to get to bed (sleep is another matter) early the night preceding a flight before the crack of dawn. Perhaps more important, I take it easy and try to get some good rest (and, I hope, sleep) as soon as I can, following my brutal travel day. Moreover, I pay the price when I don't get proper amounts of rest, and being sick—either briefly or especially long-term—can be a major drag on your travel enjoyment. I know; I have been there.

I discuss relatively extensively eating and drinking while traveling in chapter 7. Now, however, I want to focus on the importance of water consumption. Once again, the best advice is the most simple: stay hydrated. Of course, this is especially important in hot arid places like the Outback in Australia, but it is also extraordinarily important if at high altitude (e.g., the Inca Trail or other mountainous locales). Running low on H_2O can bring on headaches, nausea, fatigue, heat prostration, and worse. And here's the kicker: Sometimes water alone is not enough. You have to keep those electrolytes up, and this may require water and at least occasional supplements of sodium, potassium, and calcium.[8] Without getting too complicated at this point, let me just make the point. Stay hydrated by consistent sipping. Avoid the error of waiting until you are thirsty and then gulping down a bottle of water.

Eating is also something I will take up in more detail later. For now, I think my most helpful thoughts can be summed up in one word—balance. If possible, several relatively light,

---

[8] Be sure to discuss *any* new supplement regimen with your doctor before you begin your journey.

well-balanced meals (i.e., appropriate amounts of proteins, fats, carbohydrates) seem to work best for most travelers. A water drinking analogy is helpful here. The answer to eating well is *not* waiting until you are famished and then knocking down a three-thousand calorie meal. Nutritious snacking is a good way to go. In fact, many experienced travelers rely on protein bars for sustenance during a busy day. I am not a big fan of these because of their normally high saturated fat content, even though recent reports seem to indicate that some forms of saturated fat may actually be beneficial. I do think fruits that can be pealed and hard boiled eggs (just the whites for me, please) when available make for nutritious, healthy snacking.

Okay, as long as we are talking about putting stuff—preferably healthy stuff—in your mouth, let's talk briefly about your teeth. Most of us from time to time use our teeth for something other than chewing our food and helping with our speech. We know that our jaws are strong and our teeth can be excellent grippers of just about any kind of surface, so we find all kinds of creative (and bad) ways to use our teeth—nail biting, chewing ice, tearing open packages, pulling corks out of wine bottles. The list of teeth abuse is endless, limited only by our imagination and the degree to which we wish to be foolish. My point is that any time you use your teeth for *anything* but speech and chewing food, you are taking a totally unnecessary risk of injuring your gums or a tooth and, in doing so, risking your day, your week, or even your whole trip. Let's face it, repairing a broken canine tooth while you are trekking through the mountains of Madagascar is not going to happen, and having to live with that broken tooth for any time at all is certainly a stressful, unpleasant experience—at best. Point made.

And while we are on the topic of dental care, I need to run

the risk once again of stating the obvious: Be sure to maintain your dental hygiene by brushing and flossing as often as you reasonably can. This practice should not prove to be difficult to maintain. Just stay the course and don't be foolish. This, however, is easier said than done for some of us, I suppose.

Before I close this very important chapter, I need to make a few more points relating to safety and health, specifically, prevention and maintenance. First, a word about smoking. No lectures at this point. The health risks as well as the expense and the negative impacts on others are well known to all of us. Just remember this: Traveling—especially on extended, multi-country trips—is *much* less complicated if you don't smoke. If you are reading this as part of planning your itinerary, say about three months or so from your departure date, and you are a smoker, please consider this to be a superb time to quit. Also, while enjoying a couple of glasses of wine or a cocktail or two is something many of us enjoy, my advice is to drink alcohol in moderation—especially when you are out and about for the evening and *most* especially if you are not with a group. And finally this: Never, *ever* have *anything* to do with illegal drugs—*never!*

Be sure to remain on schedule with your meds and supplements. Pack a small first-aid kit which includes disinfectant[9], a few bandages, meds for upset stomach, cotton swabs, adhesive tape, and some form of mild pain reliever. Sunscreen and insect repellant with DEET are musts in many locations. Malaria prophylaxis is *absolutely essential* in some regions and must be taken assiduously. For those of us with knee or ankle issues, wraps and supports can make hiking and climbing

---

[9] Never neglect cuts, scratches, and blisters no matter how minor they may appear to be.

much less difficult. Walking sticks can also prove to be very helpful, if not absolutely necessary, for difficult going such as the Inca Trail in Peru. Stay well, and your chances of having a really fulfilling, low stress adventure of a lifetime will be increased dramatically.

Chapter 7

Eating and Drinking

W hile eating and drinking can be two of the most enjoyable aspects of life, ingesting tainted substances can be unpleasant, harmful, or even deadly. So care and common sense—not paranoia—need to be applied one hundred percent of the time. Let's talk some more about water first, since the rules for its consumption are a little less complicated than those pertaining to food.

I recommend that you try to keep at least a half-liter of fresh clean bottled water with you at all times—no matter where you are during your travels. It is extremely important to be confident about the *source* of your bottled water. Some street vendors will attempt to sell you unsafe water in resealed bottles. So check those seals. As for tap water, unless you are *certain* that the tap water is fit to put in your mouth and that it will not make you sick, do not use it—not even for brushing your teeth. I do solicit and trust information about water safety from the folks who work at the reception desks of lodges and hotels. After all, business is not going to be good for places that poison their guests. If, however, the hotel staff informs you that the tap water is satisfactory for brushing your teeth but not for drinking—as was the case the last time I visited Hong Kong—I take the extra precaution and avoid using the tap water in either case, although many travelers are not concerned about using tap hotel water for teeth brushing. When having meals at hotels or restaurants catering to international clientele, once again the wait staff and the hosts can be trusted for guidance on the suitability of the water (including ice for drinks). Remember the rule: Avoid taking unnecessary risks. When traveling in most Asian, African, and South American countries, it is wise to assume that tap water is not safe for anything other than bathing. And once again, no matter where you are, do not be afraid to ask a responsible party about water suitability. Trust me, they have heard the question before. Just remember to be as tactful as possible when asking such questions; there is no reason to be insulting about this.[10]

As for other beverages, I have found that commercially manufactured bottled wine and especially beer can normally be trusted, but mixed drinks and juices perhaps not so much. Coffee and tea never presented any problems for me. Ultimately, you need to trust your gut feelings (no pun intended) as well as your careful use of risk management.

Eating poses greater challenges, I think, than drinking. The main complicating factor is that there are no guarantees food will be prepared safely the way that, say, properly bottled

---

[10] Also remember that you can usually make your own safe drinking water if you have a means to boil most water for at least five minutes. Once again, use your common sense about the types of water you choose for boiling. Some water simply isn't suitable under any but absolutely dire circumstances.

water almost always is. That said, common sense and caution—not paranoia—are your guidelines. Taking the advice of your travel agent and your guides, as well as timely consultation with resources such as the CDC, is a good practice. Almost all reliable sources will warn against eating any raw fruit or vegetables that do not have a removable skin. Bananas, apples, or oranges that you peel yourself are probably going to be fine. Traditional salad ingredients such as tomatoes and lettuce, on the other hand, are problematic and should be avoided in many places, unless they come from highly trustworthy sources.

The other major issue about eating is the *type* of food that is being offered and the manner in which it is prepared. Spices, sauces, unusual items, foods that you are unaccustomed to eating can all be problematic. Also, keep in mind that some cultures' conceptions of "cooked" food may not be the same as those of western cultures. Moreover, you can't simply avoid eating, and you can't be reckless if you want to stay healthy, so try for *balance*. Of course, balance is the key to just about all components of a fulfilling life, isn't it?

If you are a vegan, vegetarian, or you have other specific dietary requirements, please don't let that keep you off the road. Discuss your needs with your travel agent, do your research, and plan ahead. Do your best to let your hosts and guides know about your dietary requirements as far in advance as possible. Consider traveling with a few easy-to-pack emergency provisions, and try to be as flexible (within reason) as you can be. If you are a vegetarian, for example, perhaps an occasional hard-boiled egg or two would not be straying too far from your regimen. I have spent time on the road with quite a few folks who have very specific dietary requirements, and not one of them had significant issues with eating.

The bottom line for taking in food and drink is paying attention and maintaining reasonable caution—all of the time. There are, of course, no guarantees that you will not be sickened by something you eat or drink, but, as in all things involving risk management, you can keep the odds heavily in your favor if you remain vigilant. On another personal note, while traveling I have consumed a wide variety of wonderful foods and drinks, many of them local. I have been cautious but not unreasonably so. As I write the rough draft of this chapter on 5 December 2013, I have visited over thirty countries and every continent since late January, and I have yet to be even mildly sickened by food or drink. Knock on wood!![11]

---

[11] And as I now edit and prepare the final draft of this guide, I can report that my diligence and a bit of good luck paid off: I had no issues with food or drink during my journey!

Chapter 8

Security

As is the case with many of the other topics in this guide, security could easily be the subject of an entire book—and, in fact, it is. Such publications may well be worth a look. I will leave it to you to research this topic further on your own. For now, however, I will start with this thought: You can exercise every reasonable precaution with respect to eating and drinking and other aspects of traveling deliberately, but if you are not vigilant with two key security components you may find yourself agonizingly inconvenienced, in serious danger, broke, or in any combination of these unhappy situations. To assure yourself of the most fulfilling and least stressful trip, you must *always* take care to protect yourself and your valuables.

I have already touched upon the importance of using the buddy system, and you can use it even if you are traveling solo. This does not mean that you should be afraid to take a solitary walk during the day in a safe section of town as advised by guides, concierges, and travel agents. On the other hand, improve your odds of remaining safe by keeping the risk as low as practicable. Know when you *need* to have someone covering your back and, when the need is there, know and trust that person. Oh yes, there really is safety in numbers—to avoid dangerous confrontations with nonhuman animals in the brush and with human animals in town.

Let's start with the most important component of security: your own personal safety. I am not going to belabor any particular point here. I'm just going to touch on some things that you must bear in mind. The first one is to avoid known trouble spots and generally dangerous countries in the world. You can turn to several resources for guidance on this. The United States Department of State website, your travel agent, and even the news will all prove to be very helpful. A simple understanding of current world affairs is certainly enough to get you started. And this can work two ways. You certainly do not want to mindlessly place yourself in a dangerous locale, but on the other hand you don't want to needlessly avoid a country based on a mistaken notion that it is likely hostile. Three countries serve to make my point. Somalia is largely lawless and extremely dangerous—for anyone. In terms of personal safety, it is simply a nonstarter. Iran is a fascinating country with much to offer, even though you might be led by the media to believe it should be avoided for security reasons. While I would certainly pay close attention to every detail of a trip to Iran, I would not hesitate to go there as things now stand. Then we have a country like Egypt—a highly desirable but scary place recently. Here once again, as with any country in turmoil, risk management is especially important. Check with your travel guide, State Department advisories, and other resources,[12] and after careful due consideration, make your own call. For me, the answer for Egypt would be temporary (I hope) postponement. So do keep Egypt high on your list of countries to visit, but hold off until things settle down just a bit more.

For more routine daily personal security practices, consider the following:

- Employ the buddy system whenever possible.
- Balance your desire to explore new and unusual places with your knowledge of safe, fringe, and unsafe areas.
- No matter where your wandering takes you *always* know how to get back to your home base.
- Avoid provocative language or behavior of any kind. Remember that you are a visitor and, unless you are with close friends who are residents of the country you are visiting, keep your social, political, and cultural opinions to yourself.
- Avoid excessive use of alcohol when out and about; the first thing affected by alcohol consumption is your judgment.
- Carry some mug money. This is tied to security of your possessions. While you may decide that using a money belt may be the best way to protect cash and credit cards, you should still keep *some* cash (say $10-$20) readily available in case you are ever mugged. Freely giving up a few bucks to someone who means to relieve you of some of your wealth can avoid further

---

[12] See, for example, "Security While Traveling" by ENISA (European Network and Information Security Agency) at www.enisa.europa/publications/archive/security.

confrontation and frustration from a robber who may not have an issue with hurting you.

- Leave your expensive and sentimentally important jewelry at home; carrying these items with you creates unnecessary security issues.
- Having your sunglasses at the ready allows you the very useful option of limited eye contact.
- Take time to learn at least a few key phrases in the local language.
- Be mindful of local pedestrian rules. Many cities are notorious for their drivers, who view pedestrians more as targets than as precious life forms. Activities like jay-walking, walking in the street, going against the light, and especially not carefully checking *both* directions of traffic are extremely dangerous, especially abroad. (And never forget that, for many countries, the left side of the road is the "right" side for vehicles.)
- Resist the temptation to be distracted by personal electronic devices such as iPods and mobile phones, especially while walking.
- Watch your step.

Possession security may not be as important as personal safety, but of course it is of great concern. A stolen wallet or passport can certainly ruin your day, your week, your entire trip, or worse. Here are some precautions that lower your risk of becoming a victim of theft. Leave your family jewelry, expensive watches, and other valuable nonessentials at home. Use hotel safes whenever available. Have a close look at the type, quality, and permanent placement of the safe in your room. If common sense and close examination of the safe give you a warm and fuzzy feeling, I would suggest you use it for extra cash, your passport when not needed while you are out and about, and other items such as iPads, cameras, and other expensive items that would be difficult to replace. Don't *ever* leave any of these kinds of things lying about unprotected. If there isn't a safe in your room or if what is in the room seems inadequate for any reason, you may want to work out an agreement with registration by which they allow you use of the hotel safe. After making an inventory of your valuables with the hotel manager, get a signed and dated receipt. Secure the items in a tightly sealed envelope with your signature and the date written across the seal. And while we are thinking about the front desk, I would suggest that you consider leaving your key there when you go out.

When it is necessary to carry cash, credit cards, and other items that you would usually carry in a wallet or purse, use a money belt. If for some reason you find yourself without a money belt, your least unsafe place for carrying a wallet is probably in the front right pocket of your pants. That said, while I was staying in Buenos Aires, I spoke with a man from Ireland who told me his wallet had been stolen from that very spot. Some of the pickpockets out there are really quite skilled, so always be on the alert, and don't forget to take and *use* a money belt.

Small backpacks are very useful for packing a few things for a day wandering about town. If all that you carry are the necessary basics such as water, sunscreen, insect repellant, and a power bar, go ahead and wear the pack on your back. However, if you find yourself buying a few gifts and souvenirs, turn the pack around and make it a front pack. It will look kind of dorky, but this is a much safer way to carry your precious purchases. And never *ever* put your wallet, passport, or other important possessions that are easy to pilfer in your pack—back or front.

Make a habit of storing and carrying items in the same place every time. Always return things, especially valuables, to their proper places *as soon as you have finished using them.* Losing something may be less traumatic than being robbed, but if it is lost, the item is gone just the same. Consequently, stress and blood pressure sky rocket while fun and fulfillment plummet.

Chapter 9

Pay Attention!

A fundamental component of security—of person and of property—is paying attention to *everything*. As a matter of fact, this topic could have been a subsection of the previous chapter, but I decided to devote a separate chapter to the discipline of paying attention because of its importance to every aspect of long-duration, multi-country travel. After all, paying attention to what is going on within you and around you is really what traveling and living deliberately are all about, right?

Since I am utterly convinced that fitness and general health are so important to a low-stress, high-fulfillment trip, I would like to start with this: Pay attention to your body and to your mind. Listen to what your body and your mind are telling you. Hunger, thirst, exhaustion (mental and physical), stress, and lack of sleep do not occur in a vacuum; they provide clues and warnings. Pay attention to these. Doing so could save you some serious hassles and pain, and possibly your life.[13]

By now, you know that I am a firm believer in the value of ear plugs. Their beauty is that they muffle undesirable sounds to a tolerable level, but they don't keep *all* sound out. You don't want to block all external sounds when you are out and about any more than you want to walk through a city blindfolded. Experiencing the sights, sounds, smells, and even surfaces of your surroundings doesn't only enhance your travel dramatically, but using *all* of your senses to the maximum extent possible will also help keep you safe. In other words, *keep your iPods and cellphones stowed away,* especially when moving about abroad.

When you are out and about, keep track of your surroundings. Know where you are, where you have been, and how to get back to your home base. In other words, take the necessary precautions to avoid losing your bearings or getting lost. This seems really basic and simple, but it is easy to be distracted in new and different places. Getting lost can be very stressful and often dangerous.

Make a note of or figure out ahead of time the distance

---

[13] My Africa experience provides a good example. In April I became rather ill with a serious virus. I had a fever, body aches, and a bad cough. I was very weak. While resting up in Mozambique for a few days, I noticed a large lump in the groin on my right side. It was sore to the touch. I thought I might have given myself a hernia from all of my hard, sometimes violent coughing. I got right on this and notified Mark, who arranged for me to be taken to the emergency room at a Johannesburg hospital during a long hold over between flights. You can imagine what was going through my mind. Would I need surgery? Would I have to stop my trip? As it turned out, the problem was a very swollen lymph node. I had a serious infection that required a heavy dose of antibiotics. I recovered and continued my travels. My point here is that I would not have fared so well had I not been paying attention and responded immediately to my body's signals.

and duration to and from key places (for example, travel time to and from the airport). Always establish at least an approximate cost for *all* taxi trips and try to use established, official cabs every time you need one.[14] Whenever you pay for anything, be sure to double check your change, and make sure that the credit card that is returned to you is *your* credit card. Pay attention to exchange rates, and be selective when choosing someone to provide local currency. In Argentina, for example, the official exchange rate (as of December 2013) was approximately six pesos to one US dollar, and while the rule is very rarely enforced, unofficial money changing is against the law. While so-called "blue" marketers were offering rates of ten to one and even better, they are not regulated. Consequently, theft and counterfeiting and other rip offs are not uncommon.

I have already commented on keeping close track of your stuff, especially valuables and items that you rely on. This is especially important on travel days. I have developed a routine that almost guarantees that I won't leave anything behind. Aside from checking and double-checking the large items as I pack up well in advance, I wear virtually the same clothes every time I catch a plane or a train or any other mode of transport. Wearing my hiking boots saves lots of room and weight in my

---

[14] This is advice that I can now provide because of a couple of unfortunate experiences that I had, one in Budapest and one in Buenos Aires. You would think I would have learned my lesson the first time, but I did not. Why not? Because I was not paying attention and consequently was significantly overcharged each time. I did protest to the extent that seemed reasonable, but I blew it and I knew it. So I shook it off and moved along. On the other hand, I did score an hour-long, picturesque albeit circuitous drive through Bangkok from the train station to my hotel for about ten bucks one time. My driver became lost but honored the agreement that we made on the fare *before* I entered the taxi. Get that fare established before you climb in!

backpack, and my travel jeans are comfortable and simple. The key, however, is my shirt. I always wear my khaki safari shirt. It is extremely comfortable as an outer layer in almost any kind of weather, and it has two large chest pockets. In the left pocket, I *always* place my reading glasses and my earplugs. The right pocket is *always* home for a clip-on pen, any meds I may need, and my passport. If there is any chance that I will need sunglasses (which is usually the case), they go on a cord around my neck. Camera, cell phone (if I have one with me), iPad, chargers and cords, a change of underwear, and *always* at least a week's supply of meds are placed in the compartments of my small carry-on backpack. Key travel documents, pens, writing tablet, extra reading glasses, ear plugs, calling cards, local travel information/guides, and maps are kept in my carry-on valise/briefcase. I *always* check to see that everything is in its proper place. I *always* pay attention to this. I virtually never lose anything or leave anything behind.

Follow the instructions of travel advisors and guides. Their livelihood depends on keeping you safe and happy. And pay close attention to reasonable travel precautions. Wearing your seat belt—even on buses when they are available—is always a good idea. Hang on to your boarding pass stubs until you are through passport control and customs. Pay attention to and respect all nonhuman animals. In addition to simply doing the right thing by treating all of these beings with respect, keep your hands off them[15] and do not feed them. By all means, pay attention to them; they are absolutely full of wonder!

---

[15] As far as the most pesky critters like the tse-tse and other types of flies, mosquitos, gnats, and cockroaches are concerned, my view is that you should feel free to take whatever preemptive measures that you deem appropriate—with all due respect, of course.

Finally, pay attention to the weather. I know, I know … forecasts are not infallible, but I still like the odds of having a clue about what the pros think is in store for us when we travel. Dress, food consumption, water intake, and a variety of precautionary steps can and should be taken with an eye toward the weather. Paying attention to it will save you hassles and will increase the odds of keeping you safe, comfortable, happy, and fulfilled. Once again, the idea here is to travel and live deliberately by *paying attention.*

Chapter 10

When in Rome ... [16]

St. Ambrose, who is credited for originating the wise advice that serves as the title for this chapter, had it right.

Respecting the cultures and lifestyles of the people and nonhuman animals that inhabit the places that you visit is essential to traveling deliberately and being a good guest. My purpose in this chapter is to drive home a point about behavior in and expectations of different cultures while you are out and about, and you need to prepare for this in advance. Let's start with this: Keep your voice down, your smile at the ready, and your flexibility in place. That said, don't stand for foolishness or hostility. Above all try to *be patient*. There are many resources out there that can provide very useful information on *how* to travel. I think that I would start, however, with an overview on travel—a wonderful, enlightened work by

---

[16] The original translated adage goes something like this: "If you should be in Rome, live in the Roman manner; if you should be elsewhere, live as they do there."

the renowned (and *deliberate*) journeyer, Rick Steves, entitled *Travel as a Political Act.* The book focuses on Rick's extensive travels in and knowledge of Europe, but you can apply his insight and wisdom to virtually any place. I am not going to provide a summary of his book here. I really want you to read it during your travel preparation period. What I will do, however, is to provide my own take on "When in Rome ..." with a tip of the hat to Rick and his approach.

Find a trustworthy source that will provide you with information about your destinations that goes beyond places of interest, good hotels, and day trips. Take a dive into the history, culture, political structure, festivals, foods, pastimes, and language of the places you intend to include in your travels. Try to learn some key phrases that will make you and your hosts feel a little less uncomfortable about your being in some place that is, well, foreign. Specifically, figure out how to say hello, good day, good night, please, thank you, excuse me, I am sorry, pleased to meet you, etc. You may be agreeably surprised to see how the ability to communicate in very basic terms in a pleasant, soft voice coming through a smile can greatly enhance your travel experience—and your hosts' willingness to welcome you.

Also, remember that your clothing choices, body language, and tone and volume of voice all matter. In some cultures, especially in Arab and other Asian countries, keeping a low profile is never a bad idea. You certainly don't want to appear ashamed of where you are from, but blending in a bit can be very helpful and wise. Loud clothing, booming voices, and any sort of even borderline obnoxious behavior will not win you friends in many cultures. Additionally, some cultures are very concerned about saving face. If a mistake is made by a guide, a hotel staff member, or a waiter, the way that *you* respond can have a profound impact on the ultimate impact of the error. Be quick to smile, keep your expectations reasonable, keep your voice down, be patient, and breathe deeply.[17] Remember, you are the guest and you are on holiday. Civility in everything you do is the epitome of traveling well and traveling deliberately.

I need to talk to you a bit now about street vendors.[18] Some of them, in a wide variety of places, can be very tenacious, if not downright aggressive. You can reduce the risk of difficulties with overly insistent vendors by knowing where and when you are likely to encounter them and what to do when confronted. For starters, try to avoid going alone, and do not hesitate to wear sunglasses. One-to-one, eye-to-eye contact with a tenacious merchant can be extremely stressful and may ruin your day or even worse. Some guides will tell you to simply ignore all sales pitches on the street or at travel stops—*always*. I think this is a rather draconian approach that can lead to bad feelings or missed opportunities to score a good deal on some item that may really appeal to you. Besides, I am simply not comfortable with totally ignoring the presence of another person who is attempting to communicate with me, although I am *not* going to engage with anyone who is obviously drunk or outwardly aggressive. My mantra for dealing with any such unwanted encounter is "Just say no ... thank you" in the local language. This basic, respectful approach is effective most of the time, but at times it is not. If an exceptionally aggressive vendor will

---

[17] And another tip seems appropriate to mention here: Remember that most cultures are not as tactile as American culture tends to be. While a hand shake is usually okay, back-slapping and *any* touching of a person of a different sex—especially in Arab cultures—is simply not acceptable.

[18] You can apply virtually everything I say here to panhandlers as well.

not leave you alone, keep moving if you can. But if the vendor's behavior is really over the top, unreasonably annoying, or possibly involves his or her putting a hand on you, you may use a little trick I have applied on a few particularly tense occasions. Lower your sunglasses, look sternly over the tops of the lenses, and directly into the eyes of the vendor, raise your voice *slightly*, and say *no!*. Having an escape route in mind is an especially good strategy during such an episode. So far, so good. I have had three successful escapes with no escalations using this approach.[19] I'm not making any guarantees here, so paying attention, using your very best judgment, and trying to avoid difficult situations like these in the first place are all essential.

Let me finish with some thoughts on the tricky subject of tipping. Most Americans are very familiar and comfortable with tipping waiters, taxi drivers, housekeeping folks, bellmen at hotels, and even the guy who wipes off your seat at a ballgame. It is part of our culture, and it is our way of offsetting the generally low pay of service personnel. In some countries, however, tipping is not expected and in a few places it is considered to be an insult. So there is a balance to be struck here. The question becomes "How do I avoid being a cheapskate without tipping too much or offending those who assist me?" I am fairly confident that I struck the proper balance by working closely with both my travel agent and my on-location guides. My basic rule is as follows. If you have determined that tipping is accepted or expected in a particular locale, consider

---

[19] I should note here that any time you *genuinely* fear that you may be harmed—and paying close attention will help you make a reasonable determination—do not hesitate to call out for help. No one may immediately come running to assist you, but the disturbance alone will probably get the aggressor to leave you alone. I know this option may seem to be a bit of an overreaction, but your personal security trumps just about every other consideration.

$3 to $10 per trip for transport (depending on distance), ten to twenty percent to wait staff (depending on the quality of service), $2 to $10 for luggage handling (depending on the weight and number of bags), and $5 to $30 per day for your guide (depending on the challenge and length of the day). Remember that tipping is always discretionary. It is usually appreciated. It is not an exact science but more of an art form. The key here is to balance your generosity and appreciation of good service with a real understanding of local custom and respect for those who assist you.[20]

---

[20] When you wish to photograph individuals, there are three important things to keep in mind. Always ask for permission first; be prepared to pay; and *always ask for permission first!*

One of my greatest challenges in assembling this book was deciding which photos to include. I had to be very selective. After all, this is not a photo journal. So I decided to go with a representative sampling arranged by continent in alphabetical order. Perhaps you will see some of the themes of my narrative within a number of these images. In any case, I hope that they, along with the other parts of this book, may move you to plan and then embark upon at least one sensational journey of your own.

AFRICA

Hakuna Matata

Mora Mora With A Lemur In Madagascar

Beautiful And Vast Lake Malawi

The Timeless And Exotic Sphinx

A Township Elementary School Class In South Africa

Nelson

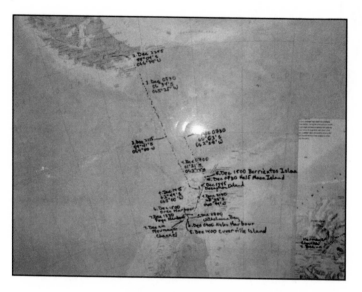

ANTARCTICA

Late Spring In Antarctica

Rock Of A Thousand Faces

Exploring By Zodiac

Mountain Climbing In Antarctica

ASIA

From A Sunset On The Beach In Maldives …

…To An Early Evening in Dubai: What A Difference A Day Makes!

The Splendor Of The Turkish Countryside

Flag Of Flowers Near Ataturk's Tomb

AUSTRALIA AND NEW ZEALAND

Cape Reinga-Where The Tasman Sea,
The Pacific Ocean, And Spirits Come Together

Fly Fishing Near Lake Taupo, NZ: No Catch; Who Cares!

Wombat Crossing Near Cradle Mountain, Tasmania

Uluru: A Quietly Spectacular And Very Spiritual Place

EUROPE

The Really Tight Fit At Novi Sad, Serbia

Trevi Fountain, Rome

A Springtime Hike In The Alps-Near Wengen

Santorini - A Must When Visiting Greece!

NORTH AMERICA

Floatplane Flight From Yellowknife To Blachford Lake, NT, Canada

My Beloved Vancouver

Near A Salmon Monitoring Station-Whitehorse, Yukon

Prince Edward, Island, Canada

SOUTH AMERICA

Buenos Aires

Moai: Rapa Nui (Easter Island)

Iguazú Falls, Argentina

Futaleufú River, Patagonian Chile

The Jewell At The End Of The Inca Trail: Machu Picchu

Lake Titicaca, Bolivia

Old Friends At The End Of The Journey

Chapter 11

Weather

I was tempted to include my comments and advice pertaining to weather in chapter 16, which, among other things, deals with flexibility and acceptance, since they are so important to keeping stress levels down and fulfillment levels up as you wander in the wonders of the world. The simple fact of the matter is that you can't do anything to change the weather any more than you can change the cultures of the various places that you visit. So, live with it, appreciate and enjoy what you can, adapt, and most of all, be ready mentally and physically.

Often, points are best made by using examples. Here are mine. When I was in the itinerary-planning stage of my travel preparations, I worked closely with my travel agent Mark to follow moderate weather patterns. Starting out in Hawaii in January and then New Zealand and Australia in February and March made perfect sense. Getting started with my two-and-a-half month African segment from April 1 through early June also worked—except for one potential problem in particular.

My itinerary had me headed to Tanzania, one of the real gems of my travels, in what is normally part of the rainy season. I was thoroughly briefed by Mark and knew that by scheduling my Tanzania visit for that time of year I risked spending my entire time there under a constant downpour. So I prepared myself mentally for that possibility, which meant having no unrealistic expectations of clear blue skies and mild temperatures for some of the best animal viewing in the world. And I prepared physically by carrying my waterproof backpack and bringing along good quality rain gear and plastic bags for cameras and other sensitive items.[21] (By the way, I did *not* pack an umbrella!) I believe that I was thoroughly prepared for dealing with just about anything Mother Nature had in store for me, so you can imagine my utter glee when day after day I was treated to clear skies and temperatures in the mid to high twenties (Celsius). I caught an enormous break, as rainy weather preceded and followed my visit to Tanzania. The farmers were quite pleased with the seasonal precipitation amounts, and I was thrilled with the wonderful weather that graced my time at Ngorongoro Crater, Oldupai Gorge, and the Serengeti!

One the other hand, my August visit to Whitehorse, Yukon, with the primary goal of viewing the Northern Lights early in the season was filled with rain—day and night. Nevertheless, I did have a two-hour window one night about an hour and a half outside of town to watch the lights and be amazed. I was ready for the window of fair skies, thoroughly enjoyed every moment in the wonder, and was thankful for what I was able to experience. Sure there was some disappointment, but not much really—mainly because I kept my

---

[21] Each of these items is easy to pack and should be included for *any* long-term, multi-country travel.

expectations reasonable. Also, I hedged my bet. Just prior to heading to Whitehorse, I stayed up quite late on several nights and into the early morning hours while I was at Blachford Lake east of Yellowknife in the Northwest Territories. I was rewarded for doing so with some fabulous—and relatively unexpected—time viewing the Lights. The point is clear. Be flexible, be prepared (mentally and physically), and always be ready to focus on the wonder in *any* moment.

Chapter 12

Communication— Language and the (Almost) Constant Fog Surrounding Foreign Travel

Have you seen the Tom Hanks movie, *The Terminal*? If you have, I think you already have an idea of where I am headed in this chapter. If you haven't seen the movie, you need to. Make it part of your trip preparations. 'Nuff said.

When you think about it, is there anything more important to enjoying life completely and deliberately than communication? Giving and receiving love, sharing beauty, experiencing the wonder of new places and new things, and grasping—even momentarily—the essence of life are all functions of communication. Communication is, of course, what connects us to others, to our environment, and to ourselves. And, let's face it: language is at the heart of communication.

Attempting to define language is an endeavor that really smart, sensitive people have struggled with since ... well, since there have been people, I suppose. A smile or a shrug can be as effective at communicating a basic concept as the spoken word, if not more so at times. But I think most of us would agree that the spoken and written *word* is what does most of communication's heavy lifting.

So why, you may be asking, is the topic of communication and language relevant to a travel guide? I will answer that question with another one. Other than having and maintaining good health, what could be more important—especially when traveling to new and unique places—than understanding and being understood? One might think that the key to communication is sharing a language. Fair enough. But what exactly does it mean to share a language? Well, therein lies the rub. I think it is fair to say that, even though linguists and others have made attempts to create a universal language, these attempts have simply not accomplished their goal.[22]

For a number of interesting historical, economic, cultural, and political reasons, over the last century English has steadily become a sort of *de facto* universal language. Almost everywhere in the world, if English is not the first language, it is often the second, or at least it has some presence, especially within the sphere of people involved in the travel industry. The catch, however, is English *proficiency*. I can't tell you how many times I have fallen into the trap of miscommunication

---

[22] Perhaps the most famous and least unsuccessful of these attempts is Esperanto, the creation of L.L. Zamenhof, dating back to the late 1880s.

unintentionally set by a taxi driver, salesperson, waiter, or hotel manager who claims to speak English (and even knows plenty of words) but, in reality, is utterly incapable of *effectively* communicating in the language. Relying on an incompetent speaker's English can be frustrating and even as perilous as wandering around a new and unfamiliar city alone and at night. Consequently, part of the mystery, challenge, and fun of travel is trying to make one's way through the virtually constant fog of ambiguity that shrouds the changing landscape. That effort is made all the more mysterious and challenging, but perhaps less fun, when one cannot rely on language. Consistently assuming that a speaker's language skills can be trusted can lead to a wide range of problems and predicaments. Let me share an example with you.

Malawi is a small African country in the central part of the continent. The first language of the nation is Chichewa, but English is also used by many folks, especially those in the travel industry. While staying at an ecotourism island lodge in the very large and very beautiful Lake Malawi that comprises about a third of the country, two recent acquaintances and I decided to take a snorkeling expedition one afternoon mainly to observe and enjoy the wide variety of the lake's cichlids. I will note here that all three of us are highly proficient speakers of English. The young man who was selected to be our "guide" was taciturn as he led us over some hilly and forested land on the island to the place where our adventure was to begin. When we asked him where we should go and where we should end our swimming and snorkeling adventure, he responded in basic but *apparently* clear English that he would meet us at a beach a kilometer or so to our *left* while pointing in that direction. He also agreed to our request that he take our towels, extra clothing, and cameras to the same beach where he would be waiting. Establishing the termination point was very important because the shoreline was extremely rocky and sheer, almost impossible to climb. After asking him at least two more times about the details of our meeting place—just to be certain that the details were clear to *each* of us—we set off on our snorkeling adventure.

After about forty-five minutes of snorkeling in the increasingly turbulent water with no sign of the promised beach, the three of us huddled up in the water and tried to assess our situation. About two hundred meters ahead was a point in the island, and the youngest and strongest swimmer volunteered to swim to it and scout out a landing place. The other two of us swam to the shoreline and clung to rocks. Our scout returned to report that there was no beach as had been promised. We decided that our only choice was to swim back to our starting point. We were now all quite tired, very cold, and quite anxious. My own concerns grew exponentially when, shortly after our decision to turn around, my left leg started cramping seriously, making much more swimming a virtual impossibility. Somehow I made it back to the rocks and then struggled to find a place out of the water. I could see my companions swim around a point and out of sight. Then I waited and shivered for over an hour.

Fortunately, my companions made it safely back to our point of origin and found their way to camp, where they informed the manager of my likely location. Eventually, the searchers found me and I was united with my friends. The promised beach, we learned later, was about a kilometer and a half in the direction *directly opposite* of the one "communicated" to us by our guide.

I had a protracted discussion with the lodge manager that continued through emails long after I left the island. The focus of my correspondence was the importance of well-trained guides who were effective communicators. I was very concerned that management was not taking the matter seriously enough and that other camp visitors could be put in similar, potentially catastrophic situations. After finally receiving adequate assurances from the lodge manager, I let the matter rest.[23]

My point in taking time to relate this story is to illustrate the great importance of adequate language skills as an effective means of communicating essential information. And my advice here is to avoid making untested assumptions about a so-called English speaker's competence, especially when it comes to important directions or instructions.

I want to make another point about communication, language, and the persistent fog of ambiguity that envelopes long-term, multi-country travel. While traveling in countries where English is not the first language, I reaffirmed my conviction that what I will call *nuance* is an incredibly important part of using a language effectively. Language in general and English specifically is often highly dependent on subtleties or nuance. Think of the importance of tone and irony in everyday conversation or how the incorrect choice of a seemingly insignificant two-letter preposition can completely alter the meaning of a sentence and, therefore, the speaker's intention. All of this is

---

[23] I will add that the small beach where we were supposed to finish our snorkeling and meet our guide was almost completely blocked by the presence of three large illegal fishing boats, which were blocking most ways to enter the beach from the water. This is a point that I also vigorously made with the lodge's management team.

made even more complicated when you factor in all of the apparent craziness inherent in the spelling of many English words. Oh yes, and there are over 250,000 words in the language—far more than most other languages. Obviously, we can't suddenly create a world of proficient English speakers. How bland the world would become if we could! So what is to be done? Well, I have some ideas. When attempting to determine if it is wise to even attempt to communicate in English with someone for whom English is not a first language, I try to keep the acronym LATS in mind. It stands for *listen* (carefully), *assess* (the speaker's success of understanding and being understood), *test* (their proficiency by asking simple questions germane to the content of the conversation), and if you determine that the speaker's ability is at least fairly reliable, continue to speak, but *simplify* your speech. Please don't assume that increasing your volume will help matters. Even though many of us do this, the practice only adds to the chaos. The problem is not the other person's ability to *hear* you. To move ahead with my effort to communicate, I speak slowly and I go with very basic sentence structures, focusing on nouns and verbs. Sometimes I will mix in key words from the other person's first language—when I am certain of their use—for clarification. If, for example, you need water, don't get into a lengthy conversation about why you are thirsty, just focus on what you need. I know this sounds pretty basic, but I have witnessed many English speakers fail miserably at communication and raise their anxiety and blood pressure levels in the process by overcomplicating a request.

While we are on the topic of communication and the fog of ambiguity that often surrounds travelers in a new place and is increased by language issues, let's go back to a couple of points that I have mentioned previously—first, "When in Rome …" and second, preparation. I would urge all long-term, multi-destination travelers to attempt to learn the basics of at least one additional language. For non-native speakers of English, I would suggest that they try to develop some level of proficiency in English. For those of us who do speak English fluently or as a first language, I would strongly suggest that we work on our Spanish. Spanish is relatively easy to learn for English speakers, and it is spoken as a first or second language in a large number of countries. Think of how you could decrease the fog of ambiguity floating around your first multi-country trip to South America if you spoke Spanish fluently or even just moderately well. Differences in accents and some dialects can certainly impact but will not negate the value of your knowing another language at some level of proficiency. Argentinian Spanish, for example, differs from Mexican Spanish, but the differences are not going to create any significant impediment to communication. Go ahead and start working on a second language while you are making other preparations for your travels.

Chapter 13

Pace

As I write this initial draft, I have been on the road almost constantly since late January of 2013. The date today is 9 December 2013, and since leaving Florida on 28 January I have been in over thirty countries on all seven continents. The travel in Africa, for example, was dynamic if not manic on a few days, and there have been times that I have had just a bit too much of a good thing. Moreover, I have been absolutely exhausted on more than one occasion. The point I want to make here is related to several that I made in chapter 9 ("Pay Attention!"). You have to listen to yourself, and when your body or your mind is telling you to give yourself a break, *take one.*

Pacing yourself begins well before you hit the road. Designing your itinerary with care and an awareness of your physical, mental, and financial (PMF) limitations is essential. Once again, your travel agent can be an invaluable collaborator during this process. Mark was extraordinarily helpful as I began to make decisions on where I wished to go and for how long. He also asked me at the outset how much money I was willing to spend for airfare and other transportation, accommodations, tours, and other expenses. We discussed my fitness both physical and mental in some detail. Then we began to assemble an itinerary that was exciting and challenging yet reasonable, which meant including ample time for recharging my PMF batteries at key points along the way.

Even with intelligent, careful, *deliberate* planning, you aren't going to be able to anticipate all of the twists and turns that are waiting for you. These challenges are all part of extensive traveling; they should be expected, appreciated, and handled calmly. Of course, this is easier said than done!

Another example from my time in Africa will help me illustrate. Upon my arrival in Cape Town on 1 April, I had been traveling for just over two months in Hawaii, New Zealand, Australia, and Singapore. I was alert, physically well rested, mentally relaxed, and in excellent shape financially, having stayed well within my budget to that point. My time in Cape Town was lovely in every respect. Being able to communicate so easily in English was a key factor in making my time in this magnificent city so restful and relaxing. Additionally, I had a first-rate guide, Brahm, whose experience, wit, and wisdom were second to none. When the second leg of my Africa adventure began with my first real challenge in Madagascar—with its different languages, more rugged terrain, and less advanced infrastructure—I was PMF ready.

My Madagascar trip was even more spectacular than I had imagined it would be. The wildlife was abundant, the natural beauty of the land was truly awesome, and the people, including two American expats I met and became fast friends with, were sensational. The plan and the trip itself were humming along smoothly.

Then came my last day in the Madagascar bush and the two-and-a-half hour river ride in an open twelve-foot motor boat. I was to travel from our base camp to Tamatave, where I was to catch my plane back to the capital, Antananarivo. After a night there, I would head back to South Africa. We began the boat ride with an uncooperative motor and in pouring rain, which continued for virtually the entire trip. For Madagascar, it was a chilly day. I began to feel ill before the boat trip finally came to an end. By the time I reached the second stop of my South African adventure (a wild game park near Mozambique) I was really sick with a fever of 103°F. With the help of fellow travelers who had wisely packed cold and fever meds (which I will always pack from now on) I made it through the worst of my illness without too much discomfort and was able to enjoy my time in the South African bush. What I did not realize at the time was that I had been and continued to be far sicker than I had realized. Although I was never given an official diagnosis of pneumonia, a follow-up appointment at an emergency room in Johannesburg strongly suggested that was indeed what I had.[24] For the next ten weeks as I traveled through about a dozen countries, I was hampered by low energy, weakness, and a persistent cough. These health issues were not enough to stop me in my tracks, but I had to adapt to them and deal with them.

As I have noted previously, there was one particular episode related to my illness that seems to best illustrate the importance of pacing yourself as well as paying attention. It

---

[24] This is the same health episode that I discuss in a long note near the beginning of chapter 9 ("Pay Attention!).

occurred while I was in Mozambique just after completing my time in South Africa. At about one-thirty in the morning, I was awakened by a pain in the crease between my abdomen and my right thigh. When I instinctively reached down to the area, I felt a large lump that was mildly painful to the touch. I instantly concluded that my persistent coughing had caused an abdomen tear and had produced a hernia! Imagine my initial sleepy thoughts. Surgery back in the United States would be required, and I would have to miss all of my time in Tanzania, Egypt, and probably more. I collected myself and later that morning found a way to contact Mark. Together with the help of Mark's contacts in Johannesburg, where I had a previously scheduled layover before my follow-on flight to Malawi, we were able to fashion a reasonable plan that would get me some absolutely necessary medical attention. This move would turn out to be a trip saver.

And here is what I am getting at with respect to my illness and the importance of pacing yourself. We had intentionally scheduled a particularly long hold-over in Johannesburg between my flight from Mozambique to Malawi. We knew I would need some time to catch up with a few things. Little did we know during the planning stage, however, just how *much* time I would need! The bottom line is that we factored in the need for *pacing* for anything that might arise. In this case I was able to catch a ride to the emergency room of a hospital fairly close to the airport. I saw an excellent doctor within an hour or so. He checked me out; there was no hernia and no need for an emergency trip back to the US for surgery. Blood tests did reveal that I had a nasty infection from head to toe. The lump I had felt was a severely swollen lymph node. I made some adjustments to my travel and tour schedule, took my antibiotics, and continued to assiduously pace myself. Slowly but surely my strength returned, my health improved, and I continued to wander in the wonder. I never returned to anywhere near one hundred percent, however, until late June.

My point in relating this experience is to draw attention to the vital inter-relationship of many of the tips and practices I have mentioned so far. I want to emphasize how pacing yourself can prevent some unexpected bad surprises and can keep those that do occur from ruining your travels. Pacing yourself—physically and mentally—can keep you going even in the more difficult times, and pacing yourself financially (i.e., properly budgeting your finances) can fund the unexpected expenses that will always accompany the challenges, twists, and turns of long-term, multi-country travel.[25]

Pacing yourself, I can testify, is necessary; it is a huge component of traveling deliberately.

---

[25] The costs of the emergency room visit, antibiotics, and over-the-counter meds that I had to pay for did mount up, and for a number of reasons it was best that I paid for these in cash. The out-of-pocket expense of dealing with a significantly more serious health problem, however, would have been much, much greater. In any event, I had all of the extra cash that I needed because I had been pacing my spending.

Chapter 14

This chapter could consist of four words: "Bring plenty of dollars." But there is, of course, more to say. The key to traveling with the right amount of cash once again is being deliberate in planning and in traveling.

When I first started honing in on the specifics of my trip, I wondered about cash and whether I should bring much with me. Fortunately I checked with Mark, and he was very clear in his advice: Yes, bring plenty of US dollars. In my case, he suggested $7,000—about $1,000 in fives, tens, and twenties and the rest in large denomination new crisp bills. When you are almost anywhere outside of North America and want to use your US currency for just about anything, those on the receiving end believe new and crisp is a good hedge against counterfeit cash and adds to the desirability of your currency. There are some things that will *require* use of your US dollars. Airport arrival expenses such as visas and reciprocity fees in some countries and emergency medical expenses such as the costs of my emergency room care in Johannesburg come to mind. Often taxis, tour ships, international terminals, and duty-free shops much prefer American greenbacks. And virtually any kind of tipping can be done with US currency.[26]

You are, of course, also going to need local currency in addition to your US cash. I am going to state the obvious and then add an additional tip or two here. Be sure to bring an ATM card. I attempted to make a go of it while spending ten months in New Zealand, Australia, and Southeast Asia without one, relying on cash transfers to bank accounts that I opened in New Zealand and Australia. It was an interesting experiment, but it was clumsy, time-consuming, and stressful. Once again, bring and use an ATM card.

Exchanging US dollars for local currency can be relatively easy and painless—in Australia, for example. Or it can be a challenge. Speaking of challenging currency exchanges, let's discuss Argentina briefly since I am in that country as I write this. In Argentina exchanging money is not legal, even though you will be serenaded by a cacophony of "*Cambio! Cambio! Cambio!*" (Change! Change! Change!) almost every time you go for a walk in a commercial district. Now the official rate here at the moment is about six or seven pesos to one US dollar. When dealing with the so-called "blue market" money exchangers on the street, I could do as well as ten to one and possibly better. The problem is that since there is no regulation in the process, I could be swindled with counterfeit pesos or, worse yet, robbed. I do not exchange money this way. I go to the local information office, talk in Spanglish for a while to my friends there, and take a bit of

---

[26] I will have more to say in the next chapter about how using US currency for many purchases can actually save you money.

a hit. I walk away *safely,* however, with a fistful of pesos at a rate of about eight to one.

In this chapter and others in this guide, I am not trying to spoil all of the fun by trying to develop in you a sense of paranoia where you are always on your guard. Take these precautions as seasoned tips—safeguards that can be made more or less rigid depending on time and place and event. If you are going to do something special or high-end in a city like Buenos Aires and you will be taken by taxi to an event and straight back to your hotel, you can certainly be less strenuous in your security precautions. Enjoy your travels even when carrying cash and moving through transitional places by paying attention, which is always a good idea *anywhere* you are, and by moving about deliberately.

We have already discussed personal and property security, but I think a brief reminder is appropriate here. When possible keep significant amounts of cash (US or local currency) in your apartment, hotel, or cruise ship safe. The bulk of the cash you do carry with you should be kept in a money belt. *Do* keep a small to moderate amount of cash at the ready for both incidentals and "mug money." Purses, obvious wallets in your back pocket, jewelry, and watches (especially those with expandable bands) are all easy pickings. Carry or wear them at your own risk, but I strongly recommend that you leave the expensive jewelry and watches at home and don't carry your passport around unless it is required. In some places and for some transactions you do need to have your passport handy. For most of your business, however, a driver's license will do nicely. So, basic ID like your driver's license, a credit card, and larger amounts of cash—not your mug money—can be carried in a money belt, while small amounts of spending money are best kept in a front pocket. For those of you who like to carry a purse, feel free to carry an inexpensive one, but carry nothing in it that you cannot afford to lose. An inexpensive over-the-shoulder purse will do, but you must pay attention to it by keeping one hand in contact with it and keeping it close to your body. Furthermore, be sure to pay close attention to your purse and other bags when you stop for a meal or something to drink. No matter how well off you are financially, spending money needlessly, wasting your cash, losing it, or having it stolen is certainly stressful and can undercut the joy of your travels. Traveling deliberately includes being careful about having a plan in place for cash protection.

Being wise with your spending and your cash should begin *long* before you hit the road. Establishing a budget for each month, if not each week or even each day, of your journey and staying within it from the start will prove to be very helpful. Feel free to work on this with your travel agent or friends who have been around or both. Also, booking well in advance, traveling off peak, looking for specials, using coupons, and other common sense methods can keep money in your pocket. We will have lots more to discuss about stretching the funds in your budget in the next chapter.

Chapter 15

Bang for Your Buck

Getting the most for your money is another travel topic that could fill a book in itself. I am going to stick to some basics here, in no particular order of importance. For starters, I will take you back to the first chapter and one of the key themes of this book: careful and deliberate planning. Watching for specials, booking trips, tours, and rooms early, and teaming up with a seasoned travel agent when working out your long-term plan certainly can save you big bucks down the line.

I also want you to keep medium-term and short-term planning in mind as a way of keeping money in your pocket. By medium-term planning, I mean thinking about specific *segments* of your travels that may call for some tweaking—one day to maybe several weeks in advance. Falling in love with a particular spot and deciding to stay there for a few extra days obviously calls for some logistical maneuvering that should not throw the rest of your travels into chaos. One way that you can do this by being willing to settle for less than ideal travel times that often carry much less expensive fares and can, consequently, offset the extra expense of your extended stay. Short-term planning may actually be the most important type of planning when it comes to remaining happy with your cash flow and conserving your financial resources. Establishing the *entire* cost of an item or a service at the time of the transaction *before* money changes hands is a must. Taxi fares are an obvious example, and a service charge for the mere use of a restaurant table, which is different than a tip, is another example.

Next, check the terms and conditions of your credit card. Does it include an automatic charge for purchases made internationally? Chances are that it does. That additional two percent or so can really add up and can severely undercut any points program that you may have in place with the card and the bank that sponsors it. While traveling, I carry two credit cards. One is a Bank of America MasterCard with a good points program that I often use within the United States. For the last several years I have also carried and used—mainly for international purchases—a Capital One VISA (Venture) card. It also carries a decent points program *and* it does *not* add an automatic additional international purchase "processing" fee as do many other cards.

While we are on the topic of credit cards, I want to make sure that you realize that the banks that support your credit card will use the *official* rate of exchange when determining the amount of US currency that it will take to finalize every international purchase you make. This is especially important in countries like Argentina where the official rate and the street rate differ significantly. If you use your US cash for purchases in the markets, for example, you will often pay at a rate fairly close to what the money changers on the street are offering. Consequently, paying with US cash could give your bucks a lot more bang. Please do check to be sure that using US currency for purchases in other countries is not against the law. We don't want my money-saving tips to cause you trouble with the authorities.

When possible, walk. Know where you are heading, wear the appropriate clothing, be secure, and carry a map, water, insect repellant, your camera, and other area-specific items that you will need. Of course, walking is also fantastic exercise, and being out of a taxi and on your own feet or even in a chair if you need one will allow you the opportunity to experience the sights and sounds of the place as well as its smells, its feel, and its essence. And since this chapter is about value, safe walking is virtually always far less expensive than being moved about by some other mode of transport.

As you are walking, remember that the beautiful, showy main avenues and areas of any large city come with a price. The cost of things on Fifth Avenue, in Hong Kong's Tsim Sha Tsui, or along the Champs Elysée is simply going to be higher than it is a couple of side streets away. Do some exploring as basic safety rules and common sense dictate, and if you do decide to make a purchase, you will certainly do better just off the more obvious and glitzy routes.

As for buying things, it has been my experience to ask—even if you are in a mainstream, more conventional type of store—if the price listed is fixed. Buying two or three of an item you like rather than just one can often get you a deal no matter where you are. In some parts of the world, the asking price is merely the opening step in the dalliance between merchant and shopper. Your bargain hunting, however, should be tempered somewhat. I am reminded of a time when I was on the road to Cusco. We took a rest stop, and while there I saw some beautiful and obviously hand-made blankets for sale at a makeshift roadside stand. The proprietor and craftsperson was an elderly woman who was eager to make a sale. I asked her the price of one rug and she told me. I then asked the woman how much two would cost and she gave me a better rate for each by buying two. Could I have done even better? Sure, but would the savings of some Peruvian *soles* mean more to me than the extra profit would mean to the woman if we did no more bargaining? For me, a fair price is a fair price, and pushing downward to the rock bottom is more of an indication of being a cheapskate with a big ego than it is of being a fair and deliberate shopper. Let your conscience be your guide.

I have mentioned previously the importance of establishing the full price of transport before you even get in the taxi or whatever conveyance you are considering. This point bears amplification here. Even if you are working through an "official" agency at the airport, establish the cost of the fare before you get started. I failed to do this in Budapest and Buenos Aires when taking a taxi from the airport to my hotel, and I took a big hit each time. Also, if you do realize that you have been ripped off by a taxi driver or any other service provider or salesperson after it is too late to do anything constructive about it, take it easy. Try not to let your blood pressure shoot up or take the fun out of things for your travel companion(s) as well as yourself by becoming angry or beating yourself up over this. Try to learn from your experience, appreciate the moment, and move on.

We have already touched on the often tricky business of exchanging money, but some additional discussion is warranted here. I know that some of you may be uncomfortable with the idea of traveling from country to country with thousands of US dollars in your possession, and rates of exchange can vary a great deal even within a given venue. Since having money issues while traveling is never pleasant, let me make a suggestion. Consider using a service like Xoom.com. This is an online international money transfer service. It allows partnership with select money transfer services in countries around the world. You use it by sending funds from your US (only) bank

Money transfers are paid out in either US dollars or in local currency. There are fees associated with this service: $30 for every Xoom transaction over $1,000; $15.75 for those over $500; and $3.75 for those over $100 at the time of this writing (April 2014). Nevertheless, in the long run, you will do well to work through such a service.[27]

And now a few words about impulse buying. Some of the best purchases and most satisfying bargains I have ever experienced came when that little voice inside said, "Do it!" And I did. I can honestly say that I have sincerely regretted very few purchases that I have made on a whim. I think there are at least three reasons for this. First, there is low risk; I never impulsively buy a high-end item. Second, I trust my gut first impressions of art and gifts for friends and family; my basic notions of what is fun and truly unique are trustworthy, and I am not afraid to go with them. Third is luck. Yes, just that. I

---

[27] In Argentina—notorious for its wide variance in exchange rates—for example, you can send your US funds to "More Argentina" (Xoom's money transfer service in Argentina) for a cash pick-up using only the Internet. This process works especially well when you are staying in a given country long enough to be established to some degree. The cash pick-up of pesos or US dollars is made (in Argentina) at the "More Argentina" branch in Buenos Aires. The same basic process applies in other large cities around the world.

am a lucky guy. Obviously, purchasing items on the road is a function of risk management. However, if you establish an internal set of rules regarding a maximum amount you will ever spend on specific types of items, what sorts of things you will allow yourself to be whimsical about, and what is even possible to buy,[28] *and* you stay within those parameters, you can allow yourself a fair amount of room for impulse buying without much possibility of buyer's remorse later. I know, I know … some of you are saying, "Okay, but impulse buying with rules is a contradiction in terms and certainly not as much fun." I'll stay with my advice and just live with the contradiction.

Oh yes, please don't try to save money by being a cheapskate when in an obvious tipping situation and the service has been excellent. Most safari guides, hiking porters, staff and crew on cruise ships, and anyone else who has been of assistance rely on our willingness to offer them something beyond the basic charge.

As you can imagine, there are hundreds of ways to spend wisely and even more ways to simply blow your dough. Obviously, you have already done lots of smart things with your money and haven't made many bad moves with it or you wouldn't be planning or currently taking a long-term, multi-country journey—unless, of course, you are running from the police for some form of fraud! So stick with the native intelligence and good common sense that got you to this point. Don't forget the basics of wise spending just because you are on holiday, and try not to be a cheapskate either. Once again, bang-for-your-buck *balance* is crucial to being a deliberate traveler.

---

[28] Large items that present huge shipping issues, antiquities that may carry very high taxes and duties, and illegal items need to be left alone … period!

Chapter 16

Consistency and Flexibility—Reflections on the Beauty of Balance

I have been talking quite a bit in these pages about *balance.* It is a major theme of this book, and it is at the heart of this chapter. Simply stated, balance is essential while traveling on an extended, multi-country trip and throughout life for that matter. Balance includes a sense of purpose, while *deliberately* paying attention to what is happening around and inside you. Consistency is a closely related concept—and not to be confused with "a *foolish* [emphasis added] consistency," which, according to Emerson, is "the hobgoblin of little minds." With the need for consistency comes the equally important need for flexibility— thus balance. I'll explain by providing a couple of examples.

From my initial stop in Hawaii through New Zealand, Australia, Singapore, and South Africa, I was delighted with the smooth sailing that I had on my flights, in the airports, and moving through passport control and customs. I was thoroughly enjoying efficient ground transport to virtually anywhere I wanted to go. I was always prepared to facilitate my movements with passport, reading glasses, yellow-fever card, travel documents, and travel bag (complete with all the necessities) at the ready. And then I flew from Johannesburg to Antananarivo, Madagascar.

I was all set to continue my smooth swing through the airport in the capital city. Heck, I had even brushed up on my French (spoken by many Malagasy folks) for good measure. When we walked down the steps (which somehow just appeared at the plane) and on to the terminal, the excitement we passengers all shared—visions of lemurs, colorful chameleons, magnificent scenery, and fascinating people filling our thoughts—was palpable. We followed arrows to a large, dimly lit, and utterly drab room. It was sort of like a very old abandoned basketball arena but without the baskets or stands. And that's where we stayed, wandering aimlessly about, bumping into each other, and asking a wide assortment of rhetorical questions with no adult supervision for fifty-three minutes.

It is not that there were no airport personnel or airline staff in the "gym" with us. I counted as many as five folks at one point. But no one had anything helpful or even pleasant to say. Even my attempts to gain their friendship or at least solicit some assistance by speaking French to them went ignored.

At about the twenty-minute point, I got it. At first I smiled and, before long I was laughing ... alone. Not even Amy and Andy (the only other Americans in the room and soon-to-be-friends) were laughing yet. Here's the thing: Welcome to Madagascar! It is not worse than other countries. It isn't mean-spirited or rude. It is simply different—and much, much slower than many places. The Malagasy people even have a term for this way of Life: *mora mora* (slowly, slowly). You hear and see and feel *mora mora* everywhere in Madagascar, even when ordering and then waiting for a meal at a first-rate restaurant. I was not aware of this before I landed, but I soon figured it out. This is where flexibility is needed to balance consistency and discipline. As most of us know, it is amazing what laughter and steady deep breathing can do to help us find our balance and turn an experience that seems really annoying into something that is actually all part of the fun.

I think that some of the airport staff sensed my change of mood and my acceptance, because once we did receive some attention and direction, my forms and passport and customs check were somehow processed before anyone else's. Amy and Andy, who had also caught on soon after I did, were right behind me. The more rigid frowners and groaners were … delayed.

Are things at the airport in Antananarivo always like they were when I arrived? I really don't know. But I was glad that my pace had changed. It had become clear that I was in for an experience, a culture that was far different and truly unique. My experience in the "gym" had been a time to establish balance and a time to learn about *mora mora* specifically and travel generally. And my quest to find balance through flexibility and acceptance was extremely helpful, by the way, when I arrived in Mozambique, Malawi, Maldives, Egypt, Turkey, and about a dozen or two other places.

Now let's talk a bit more about the weather, shall we? I want to return to an example that I used earlier in the book, but with a different emphasis this time. I am referring to my

European river cruise—that *wasn't*. The rains came long and hard to Central Europe during the spring and early summer of 2013. The weather was absolutely gorgeous when I arrived in Budapest on June 13, but major changes in the plan had already been set in motion.

During my trip-planning stage, Mark and I had determined that the best way for me to see some Central European countries, including Hungary, Serbia, Bulgaria, Romania, and possibly Croatia, was by taking a river cruise (something I had never done before) on the Danube from Budapest to Bucharest. The trip that I chose was scheduled to include stops at great locations all along the river. We started in Budapest, and after spending a couple of fabulous days there (part of the cruise plan), we were taken *by bus* to the ship which was at anchor in Novi Sad, Serbia (*not* part of the plan). Simply stated, torrential spring rains had caused the Danube (which was not nor ever has been blue, by the way) to rise so much that we could not get under the old bridge that blocked our way a few hundred meters down river. So we waited and waited. I made up my mind early on to go with the flow, so to speak.

Some of the passengers became especially impatient and frustrated and were becoming angrier by the hour. They had flown to Budapest directly from their home countries (many were American) specifically for this river cruise, which, they now were arguing, should have been canceled days earlier, before they had even left for Hungary. They speculated that the cruise company (Viking) gambled that the water level would ultimately not be an issue, and, so the theory went, they lost their bet at the passengers' expense. In the meantime, the ship's staff did everything they could to keep us entertained. The passengers were offered improvised bus tours to a variety of interesting and alluring places in both Serbia and Croatia. We were treated to entertaining games and performances in the evenings. The food, by the way, was superb. Nothing the staff did seemed to improve the spirits of an ever-increasing number of unhappy passengers. Petitions were drafted when the company's initial offering (fifty percent off on any future Viking cruise) was vigorously booed by the majority at a trip status meeting on about the fourth day. There were even steps being taken by some toward initiating a class-action suit.

In the meantime, I worked out in the morning, took every tour I could, made some great new friends, ate well, drank my fair share, and had a jolly good time. You see, by now I had totally embraced the importance of a balance between consistency (i.e., paying attention, staying prepared, and taking really good care of myself every day) and flexibility (i.e., acceptance of the circumstances). I suppose one *could* argue that Viking management back in the States had made a blunder by not calling off the cruise days earlier. Nevertheless, I for one had easily found ways to have a ball, and I visited a number of places I would never have seen if things had gone according to plan.

Then the rumors of a new offer started circulating, and after days at anchor in Serbia the ship's hotel manager called a meeting to give us the news. In addition to the fifty percent discount on our next Viking cruise we had been promised, each of us was also to receive a *complete refund* covering room, board, drinks, tours, and virtually anything else (including airfare for most of the passengers) other than our individual personal expenses. I think it is fair to say that the mood of the passengers improved immediately and dramatically.

Three days later, we were able to get underway, clearing the bridge by a few centimeters.[29] Looking back at the entire experience, I must say the cruise was exciting, fun, and absolutely fulfilling for me and—when all was said and done—for most of the other passengers as well. Oh yes, just to reiterate: It was virtually free!

Obviously I'm doing a lot of storytelling here to make a simple but important point about balancing consistency with flexibility and acceptance, but I feel that relating these episodes was needed to drive home the importance of *balance* when you commit to traveling deliberately and getting the most out of your journey. Try to remember *mora mora,* and go with the flow (even when there seems to be no flow to go with). You will be on the road for a long time. Any change of plans short of a catastrophe is only a relatively minor distraction at worst and an amazing opportunity for spontaneity and discovery at best.

---

[29] There is even more to the story of our ill-fated cruise. While hauling in the anchor in the early morning hours of that day, a cable snapped and the wire struck and severely injured a member of the crew who was rushed to the local hospital. We were all concerned as he clung to life during the first few hours after the accident and through his initial emergency surgery. Some of us had already started collecting contributions from the guests for him and his family when we learned that he was expected to recover. If that wasn't enough, once we reached Romania we were required to leave the ship and board four buses to complete our journey to Bucharest. A tire on the bus on which I was traveling suffered a nasty blow out. But for the skill and cool response of the driver, the bus could have crashed. Fortunately, no one was hurt, and there were just enough seats on the other three buses to accommodate those of us from the one that was now out of commission. We reached Bucharest—safely—later that afternoon.

Chapter 17

Keeping Track

Your decision to travel extensively to many countries means that you will have almost limitless opportunities to experience an extraordinarily varied array of places and the animals—human and nonhuman—that inhabit them.

With these opportunities comes the chance to record them. I would like to spend a little time here to share some ideas that I have developed on the topic of recording what you experience. Our recurring thematic friend, balance, will once again play a major role in this discussion.

Let's talk about photos for starters.[30] I have come to the conclusion that taking a picture of everything that might be of even the most remote interest because we don't want to miss anything and because digital technology practically dictates that we can and should is not necessarily a good idea. Yet I have observed folks in a countless number of scenarios become

---

[30] I am assuming in this section that you are not a professional photographer who is traveling and taking photographs as part of your profession.

so focused on getting the shot that they miss the essence of the experience itself. Fair enough. Let's face it, for some people travel is all about photos taken and shared—trophies and prizes representing all that they have seen. But that's not for me, and my guess is that it is probably not for you either.

For me, stressing over getting "it" all on camera is antithetical to the very basics of traveling deliberately. How, for example, can you really take in and fully experience the sights, sounds, smells, and feel of the wonder of the wander if you are fixated on positioning yourself and your camera—which often may include jostling others in the process—to get just the right shots? My question is not merely rhetorical. Even the most tried and true multi-taskers simply cannot get to the essence of the moment if picture taking is a pre-occupation. If they try, they miss out.

Don't get me wrong here. This is not an anti-photo polemic. I think we would all agree that photos provide us with a tremendous opportunity to share special things with others, and they supplement the wonderful experiences that we have recorded within our minds and our hearts. Once again, for me, the word is *balance.* So be sure to keep your camera handy and well charged at all times. Some things really do need to be captured "on film." All I'm saying is that you can miss a lot by trying to photograph everything. Balance. 'Nuff said.

Keeping track of the memorable moments of your journey and recording what matters is certainly not all about photos. Make a point to write things down. You may only be inclined to scribble just a few notes here and there, but recording your *written* impressions of the people, places, and experiences that have brought you joy, wonder, enlightenment, or even fear will prove to be rewarding. Your written comments will provide great points of references for your own memories and for the stories that others will be eager and delighted to hear.

I would also encourage you to keep track of your daily expenses. Most of the big ticket items like travel via plane, train, and ship, hotel accommodations, and tours may be pre-paid and probably very easy to reference. Other things such as meals, gifts, tips, mini-trips, personal care products, or even medical care will need to be paid for as you go. Keeping track of these expenditures will help you avoid any unpleasant end-of-the month or end-of-the-trip expenditure surprises and will help you pace yourself and your spending. Your budget notes will also be a very interesting and helpful artifact of your journey as well as an invaluable planning tool for yourself, your friends, your family, and even your travel agent as further travels are contemplated.

Chapter 18

Keeping in Touch

You can assume that your friends and family will be very interested in keeping track of you. They will be concerned about your welfare and very interested in your experiences. Certainly, the photos you take will be shared online or in person with the people you care about. Fortunately, there are many other ways for you to keep in touch.

Don't forget about making the occasional call. Your mobile phone is handy, of course, but expensive to use when traveling in various countries. Consider phone cards. They are very reasonable (about twenty pesos or two or three bucks for two hours of calling from Argentina, for example) and easy to use. Sending a text is another good option. This mode of communication is just as handy as calling someone on your mobile phone. I arranged for a package with my US carrier that allowed me to send six hundred texts from anywhere in South America to *any*where for about $60.

Email is always an option, of course. Better yet, try sending postcards and letters. Yes, snail mail—complete with the local postage—may be slow and perhaps a bit cumbersome, but it is revered by young and old alike. Snail mail will always take you extra time and can even be relatively expensive in some places, but trust me, it is *always* appreciated and held dear by the recipient. Speaking of snail mail, I would like you to consider something else: occasionally sending packages home as you travel. Again, this process can be expensive, time consuming, and slow, but shipping gifts, notes, excess personal items, and other things to recipients back at home can help to keep your load light as you travel and acquire additional items that will otherwise end up on your back.[31]

Now for another brief return to the planning phase of your journey. I am going to reiterate here the importance of being certain that those closest to you know your basic itinerary and your travel agent's contact information. Also, be sure that your bank, credit card companies, and any other entity that would have an interest in your whereabouts know that you will be traveling internationally for a relatively long time. Also, do your best to automate direct deposit for pay checks, retirement payments, pensions, social security, and any other incoming funds. Bill paying (e.g., credit cards, house mortgage or rent, car payments, mobile phone) should also be on autopilot. This is probably best for most of us even when we are not on the road, but doing so while traveling is imperative for what should be obvious reasons.

---

[31] I strongly suggest that you use commercial companies (e.g., UPS, FedEx, DHL) for shipping as opposed to the postal service of the country you are visiting. They are usually more expensive, but they are much more efficient.

This brings us to *the* tough question of this chapter: Just how in touch should you be? Obviously, this is a dynamic consideration. Your response will be informed by the size and needs of your closest family members, whether or not you still have a job or business responsibilities, your own medical issues, and other factors that may limit your ability to cut loose while traveling. My status during this journey was not particularly complicated. I have no children and only two particularly close personal relationships, no business or job concerns, no house upkeep or mortgage, and no car. Breaking away was really quite uncomplicated and easy for me. I did take some time before I left the United States, however, to have a heart-to-heart talk with my sister to be clear about the circumstances under which I would return to help in emergencies involving family or friends. Those circumstances were, in fact, limited, but it was a good idea to discuss them ahead of time.

Your answer to my question in the previous paragraph should help you to decide what you want to take with you to do your long-distance touching. Of course, you certainly have options: laptop, iPad, mobile phone, or any combination of these. Once again, I urge you to keep the quest for balance in mind. Try to avoid dragging along anything (especially communications gear) that isn't really necessary. That said, you may need to bring a gadget or two to help diminish your anxiety level about work, family, friends, and financial obligations.

During my first long-term, multi-country trip (from October 2010 to 30 July 2011), I did not bring a cell phone with me. I did have my laptop, largely for working on a writing project. I decided against taking a mobile phone because I really did want to break free and to have the lifestyle that allowed me to do so. I also felt that the cost of purchasing a universal calling package from my carrier was prohibitively expensive and that constantly changing SIM cards was too much of a hassle to bother with.

I kept in touch in various ways, several of which I alluded to earlier in this chapter: Skype via my computer (which was a little iffy at times and often cumbersome, but free), Internet shops (where a couple of bucks would usually allow me all the e-mail and current events catch-up time I needed for several days or more), business office services at many hotels (which were often offered as a complimentary feature), phone cards (available just about anywhere), texting, and, of course, snail mail.

My final point is rather obvious, but I cannot ignore it. Prior to starting my most recent adventure, I became friends with lots of folks on Facebook. All I have needed has been my iPad and Wi-Fi connections, and I have been able to stay in touch directly or indirectly with most of the people who are close to me. I have enjoyed posting photos and status reports of my latest exploits while being able to "like" or comment briefly on what others have chosen to post. There has also been the option of using the messaging feature to send extensive private notes to anyone on my list of friends. Moreover, the communication possibilities via social networking are enormous.

The ability to keep in touch in a deliberate and efficient manner is something that requires planning, dedication, and, once again, balance. You have plenty of options for reporting on your experiences and whereabouts. Most important, however, make a pledge to yourself that with some regularity you will keep those close to you aware of how you are doing, what you are doing, and where you are doing it. Believe me; folks want to know.

Chapter 19

Don't Be Stupid— Some Tough Words about Important Stuff

Let's face it: Each of us has the capacity for fairly ridiculous behavior. This is not news. As a matter of fact, not so long ago the American Secretary of State quipped, "Every American has the right to be stupid." Not only do we *have* this right, but some of us choose to *exercise* it—frequently. Do yourself a huge favor, *especially* when you are traveling. Try hard to avoid being stupid.

Some definitions will help me make my point. Let's start with *ignorance*. I think we can probably agree that ignorance is essentially lack of information. Frankly, I don't have any major issues with ignorance, especially if we make a legitimate attempt to consider where our ignorance may lie and make a thoughtful choice on the degree to which we may want to fill the information void in that area. For example, I cannot speak Spanish very well, but I want to learn, so I am studying. Conversely, I do not know how to ride a motorcycle. I don't care. My ignorance of motorcycle riding will remain intact. So, once we choose what gaps in our knowledge or abilities need to be filled, we must act on those choices and then put into practice what we have learned.

Stupidity, I believe, comes in two basic forms. The first one is making the wrong choice by not learning about something we really should know about. For example, consider people who know that they have a strong possibility of becoming diabetic but refuse to learn what they can do to prevent it or how to postpone its onset. The second form of stupidity occurs when one's information gap is filled but nothing is done to put into practice what has been learned. Once again, think of the potential diabetic mentioned above who *does* make the correct decision by learning what he needs to learn about his predisposition to be diabetic but does nothing in response.

By reading this guide and by seeking information about travel and about specific places you wish to visit from knowledgeable travelers, your travel agent, and other resources, you have already moved past the first type of stupidity. You have made the correct choice to attack the void in your knowledge about traveling. You are safe … so far.

So, now that you presumably have learned some things about travel and traveling deliberately, what are you going to do with this knowledge? Are you going to put into practice what you have learned? Or are you going to ignore significant points and consequently be stupid? Let's get specific here. Based on what has been presented in these pages, what sorts of examples of being stupid come to mind? Not starting or not staying the full course of your malaria prophylaxis when traveling in areas where these meds are highly recommended comes to mind. So does carrying a thick wallet (probably full of cash) in your back pocket. So does leaving your hotel alone without having committed its name and address to memory. So does touching, feeling, taunting, teasing, and otherwise hassling nonhuman animals. So does mindlessly chattering away on your mobile phone as you disturb the peace, block the way, or do other really annoying things while distracted. So does not covering properly when sneezing or coughing. So does not listening to your body and responding to what it is telling you. So does not having a budget and staying reasonably close to it. So does not staying in touch with people who care about you. So does not asking about fares and other services *before* you jump in. So does not putting things like your passport, meds, mobile phone, and cash back where they belong. So does leaving your bags unattended while you are on the move. So does being rude to *anyone*, ever. So does being a cheapskate. So does not paying attention. So does not wearing your seat belt when one is available. So does not using a safe for your valuables whenever possible. So does not checking to be sure the credit card you handed over is the same one that is returned to you. So does suddenly slamming your airplane seat back into the legs of the person behind you. So does being unnecessarily loud. So does drinking excessively, especially at night by yourself while walking around in unknown areas.

Obviously, the potential for being stupid while traveling is virtually limitless. But simply being careful, being considerate, and always trying to do the right thing will keep the potential for stupidity in check. I'll tell you what: Just do your best to *practice* what you have learned and *enjoy*! There is an immeasurable amount of excitement, happiness, and fulfillment to be breathed in, experienced, and beheld in the world. All of it is just ahead of us, waiting. *Deliberately* finding and truly appreciating the wonder of the wander is both challenging and truly awesome. And the journey is so much easier and less stressful when you simply follow the rule: Don't be stupid.

Chapter 20

And What About ...?

This chapter deals with a number of important items that don't fit neatly into some other chapter or could be placed in at least several others or are not expansive enough to command their own. In any case, each point or comment I make here really does need consideration.

A Little More about Planning and Your Travel Agent

Let's begin this discussion at the beginning—the planning stage. As you know by now, I am a strong advocate of seeking the assistance—*lots* of it—from a travel agent who has plenty of experience, especially with respect to the countries that you intend to visit. Sometimes your ideal travel agent may not be located near you. This is by no means an issue, but you do need to plan on at least one face-to-face meeting with him or her within a week or two of your departure date. Review your trip in its entirety. Focus on any tricky connections you may have to make, particularly challenging destinations you are headed for, possible issues with currency or travel regulations, or *any* item your agent wants to draw your attention to or that you have *any* questions about. Certainly you may meet with your agent more than once, and you probably will. *But be certain to take the time to shake your agent's hand, look him or her in the eye, and establish that special bond that will assure you both that you are a* **team**.

Some Final Comments about Travel Insurance

Sometime before your final or only meeting with your agent, you will need to consider the option of travel insurance. Coverage can vary widely, so make a point of reviewing a number of plans that can cover events ranging from trip cancellation to personal injury and evacuation and even death. I will warn you right now that this type of insurance is not inexpensive. Depending on where you intend to go and for how long and how extensive you want your coverage to be, a plan for just one person may cost several thousand dollars. That said, I cannot emphasize too vehemently how much I believe in travel insurance. I strongly encourage you to do your homework and review a number of policies, with the assistance of your travel agent, fellow experienced travelers whom you know and trust, and any other resource that you feel comfortable using. When you have found a plan you like, buy it. Often it seems that if you have insurance you probably will never need it. Let's hope this is the case! If you don't have it, something will happen to make you wish you did. To illustrate, let's say you plan to visit twelve countries in Africa during a ten-week journey and have paid $40,000 up-front for transportation, taxies, hotels, etc. On day twelve, while in country number two and deep in the bush, you slip and severely fracture your ankle. You cannot walk—period. At this point, an extensive African experience is no longer in your immediate future, and without an *insured* way out of the bush via a medical flight, coverage for additional emergency medical treatment, and compensation for all of the cancellations that will have to be made, your losses are going to be mind-numbing. Wouldn't it be comforting and stress-reducing to know that this sort of unfortunate event does not have to be a total financial catastrophe? Remember, my point here is to get you into the frame of mind of doing what you can to reduce apprehension and stress and increase the fulfillment and wonder of your travels. These objectives are far more likely to be realized if you travel deliberately, and purchasing travel insurance is one important part of that way of traveling.[32]

Let People Help You

Short of serious medical emergencies, problems and unexpected needs do arise—even for the best prepared, most deliberate travelers. An important piece of gear can start to wear out or break down; issues with medicine can occur; the desire to add something to the itinerary can develop; concerns with adequacy of accommodations may become a problem. The possibilities for these types of things are endless, but there are people (guides, hotel and hostel staff, even your travel agent at

---

[32] At the time that I was writing the second draft of this section, I had just filed a trip interruption claim with my trip insurance carrier. While whitewater rafting in southern Chile toward the end of the South American component of my journey, I sustained a broken rib and other injuries that completely stopped me from participating in any further activity for the rest of my trip. For all practical purposes, my time on the river was over almost as soon as it had begun. I am delighted to say that I received a check in late April for the full amount of the policy's trip interruption coverage! Nothing could replace my time rafting and kayaking in Patagonia, but receiving the check did ease the pain.

long distance) who can help. They cannot help to make things better for you, however, if they are unaware of the issue. So inform your support team of your need for assistance without delay *and give them a chance to help*. Many trips have been saved because a deliberate traveler gave someone who could help an opportunity to remedy something which, left alone, could have become a major, possibly trip-ending, issue. I know that many of us do not wish to appear to be a nuisance or to be incapable of self- reliance. Consequently, we sometimes fail to inform those who can help us that something is just not right. Granted, sometimes keeping quiet allows what might have seemed to be an issue to simply fade away. More often, however, a traveler's silence can allow a problem to escalate to a point of no return. Communicate your concerns and save your trip.

The Fine Art of Constructive Complaining

Closely related to the preceding topic is what I call the fine art of constructive complaining. First, choose your battles carefully. When you have determined that you do, indeed, have a legitimate grievance, be selective about the best person to handle the matter. Also, pay attention to the time, place, and manner of your complaint. Be especially sensitive to local custom (e.g., the importance to some of saving face). Be clear and candid yet always tactful when stating your case. When all of these pieces are in place, be prepared to state *specifically* what you want to be done. I have rarely been disappointed when using this approach. In that rare case when this method is simply getting you nowhere, you can always politely ask to speak with a supervisor and then employ the same strategy. Also, let your reasonable concerns be known by people who can actually do something to help. Complaining to the house-keeper at your hotel about the poor service at the front desk is not the way to go. Informing your guides and hosts about your disappointment with food preparation *is*.

Luggage Tips

Once you start traveling, simply carrying on the daily basics of life changes significantly. This book attempts to address the best ways to get the most out of your life on the road while preparing for, avoiding, or dealing with the potential stressors and hassles that can arise. I can't possibly predict or discuss all of them, but I have attempted to alert you to many that I have planned for or have encountered. One of these, unmentioned until now, needs to be discussed here. I am referring to lost or damaged luggage or theft from your bags while in transit. Anytime you are in one place and your bags are in another problems can arise. The risk management component of deliberate traveling requires you to lower the likelihood of luggage issues by doing three things: limiting the time that you are separated from your bags, clearly marking each piece of your luggage, and packing with care. I was able to be a good risk manager vis-à-vis my luggage by carrying only three bags: my large backpack containing the bulk of my stuff (all of which I could live temporarily without and nothing of which was particularly valuable) that I checked when flying; my valise containing travel documents, insurance informa-tion, and other important documents; and a smaller backpack containing a change of underwear, a week's supply of meds and supplements, my mobile phone, my camera, my iPad, and anything else of value or that I considered necessary. (The latter two comprised my carry-ons.) By the way, as I mentioned previously, if you are traveling with a companion, you can cross-pack so that the loss of one checked bag can be offset by packing similar items in one another's bags. To protect against pilfering after their bags have left their control, some folks pay a few bucks at the airport to have them wrapped in plastic before they are checked. I did this only once—in Africa—because it was mandatory at one airport. I never was a victim of checked-bag theft, but go ahead and have your bags wrapped if it gives you some extra peace of mind. By the way, I also think that a typical backpack seems less appealing to a would-be thief than a fancy piece of expensive designer luggage.

Double-check to make certain that you and your checked bags are headed to the same final destination. Sometimes when you are traveling from one country to another with a layover in a third country, your bag may not be checked all the way through. You may have to claim it and re-check it to your final destination. When collecting your bag at the baggage claim area, get to it as quickly as you can. Do your best—without being pushy—to stand as close as possible to the place where the luggage first comes into view. Attaching an obvious special identifying feature like an unusual ribbon or unique decal can be helpful to you in spotting your bag and keeping others from thinking yours is theirs. If all of your diligence in staying as close as possible to your bag does not work out as planned as the carousel comes to a stop and you are still waiting, report the loss *immediately*. Carrying a photo of your bag with your contact details can be very handy when making your claim to the baggage office, especially if there is a language barrier. If you do eventually receive your bag, that's great, but be sure to give it an immediate once-over to check for any obvious damage or the possibility of pilfering. Again, report any issues of this sort to the luggage control office or police if you feel the need to do so.

Boarding Pass Stubs

I'd like to make one more point here about airplane travel. It is always a good idea to hang onto the stub of your boarding pass. When entering a new country (Egypt, for example), a quasi-official greeter will often ask to see it—even before you leave the jet way to enter the terminal. Not having your stub at the ready will really slow you down. It also contains important information like your flight number, which is often needed for visa requests and customs forms. A boarding pass stub is also proof positive for adding points or miles from your flight to your frequent flyer account. And it is always very handy when attempting to convince a large, unpleasant person that he is in your seat. I still have many of my stubs—some of which still serve yet another purpose by reminding me of some especially unusual or challenging trips.

Trains Are for Adults

We have been focusing on plane travel and airports so far in this section, but let's talk trains for a while. Here's the scoop: Trains are for adults. Once again, this is especially the case in countries where language is an issue. From baggage handling and ticket purchasing to finding the right boarding area, train car, and even seat, train travel requires more attention and self-help than easy-on, easy-off plane travel. Even finding the correct station when you are literally right on top of it can be a challenge. In Naples, for example, the station for local trains is located *under* the long-distance train station. I lost about an hour waiting in a line going nowhere before I figured it out.

There's no need to belabor my point: You must be especially diligent and on your toes when traveling by train. I love it; it is my favorite form of transport. Just sayin' … pay attention. By the way, buses can present some of the same challenges that trains present; however, in some countries (New Zealand and Australia, for example), they can be as much fun for travel as trains are.

Driving

This one is a no-brainer for me. With the exception of Canada and some countries in Europe, I simply do not drive when traveling internationally unless I have no alternative.[33] Driving a car in most other countries can be expensive, inconvenient, scary, and downright dangerous. Furthermore—and most important for me—driving a car requires you to pay attention to the *road* itself, not to all of the wonderful things *along* it. I can't tell you how many times I thought, while traveling through some gorgeous countryside by bus or train, how great it was to be transported from one fantastic place to another with nothing to do but sit back, relax, and enjoy. While on the road, do yourself a huge favor and leave the driving to others.

Laundry

On a totally different note, do your best to stay on top of your laundry. I have washed many pairs of socks, underwear, T-shirts, and other items in my hotel or hostel shower, sometimes using body wash for detergent. You never want to *pack*

---

[33] The only time that I drove a car in another country from the time I arrived in New Zealand in early February 2013 until I returned to the United States in mid-March 2014 was in Tasmania, where convenient bus and train schedules and routes were not readily available.

wet or even damp clothes, so if you have a day or two for your laundry to dry, that's great, but if you are short on time and a hair dryer is available, have at it. This is not a particularly environmentally friendly way to dry your clothes, but when used sparingly it can be a huge help. If you are staying at a hotel and you are rich or in desperate need of clean clothes or both, you can have the hotel staff do some laundry for you, usually at an insanely high price. As is the case with many low-end items like tooth brushes and toothpaste, razors, or other shaving and beauty kit items, you can almost always purchase basic clothing items (socks, underwear, etc.) at a nearby market. The local folks are always happy to make a sale.

Moreover...

Obviously this chapter could have been both highly repetitious and virtually endless. Its underlying theme is the importance of trying to stay on top of things by continually *responding* to the typical challenges of long-term, multi-country traveling instead of stressfully *reacting* to every issue—many of which can be avoided in the first place by being deliberate. If you think I have missed anything here or in the previous pages, check the index. You just may find what you are looking for there.

Conclusion

As I begin to draft this final section, I am in Buenos Aries in the apartment that I have rented for almost four months. It is a beautiful clear January day and about 32°C (around 90°F). I have been on the road for about twelve months. I am struck by where I am and the fact that *this* journey, at least, is coming to an end. In any case, I was certain from the outset that I would be writing a book that offers my best advice on *how* to travel. As I contemplated the structure of this book, I thought about what many successful writers have done when considering the organization of their works. Edgar Allan Poe and other greats claim to write their conclusions first and then aim the rest of the book toward that end. I, however, am not doing that. It has always been my intention to let this guide, including the conclusion, evolve as each day brings new lessons and material.

And so the stage is set for a caveat—actually more of a confession—that I have alluded to previously: I don't have all the answers. But you already know that. Following the best of my advice and that of your travel agent and your well-traveled friends will not guarantee that your travels will be stress-free and perfect. But you know that too. After all, this is a *guide*, not a guarantee. My guess is that you might find traveling with no challenges—a trip barren of bumps in your road—to be rather boring. In fact, I sincerely believe that those situations—so often sudden and totally unexpected—that have required me to be at my most resourceful have also enriched my travels immensely … and have provided me with the very best material for this book and for stories to share with my family and friends.

As I have mentioned several times throughout these pages, this guide is a tool to help you keep unnecessary stress and difficulties—the kinds that can be anticipated and those that really can't be—to a realistic minimum. It is designed to help you to be a thoughtful risk manager and a successful journeyer who possesses important basic knowledge about travel, a worldly sort of common sense, and the appreciation of balance to make the most out of each day you spend on the road. Have a safe and joy-filled wander in the wonder while you travel—*deliberately.*

Appendix I

Countries Visited between October 2010 and March 2014

Antarctica	Egypt*	Peru (Focus on Cusco, Inca Trail, Machu Picchu)
Argentina*	Ethiopia	Romania
Australia*	Greece	Serbia
Austria	Hungary	Singapore*
Bahamas	Indonesia	South Africa*
Bolivia (Focus on Lake Titicaca)	Italy*	Switzerland
Cambodia	Kenya*	Tanzania
Canada*	Laos	Thailand*
Chile (Focus on Rapa Nui & Patagonia)*	Madagascar	Turkey
China*	Malawi	Uruguay*
Colombia	Malaysia	Vatican
Croatia	Maldives	Venezuela
Cyprus	Malta	Vietnam
Dominican Republic	Mozambique	Zambia
Dubai/UAE*	New Zealand*	Zimbabwe*
Ecuador (Focus on the Galapagos)	Paraguay	

OTHERS

Bahrain*	Pakistan
Cuba	Panama
France	Papua New Guinea
Germany	Philippines*
Hong Kong*	Portugal
Iran*	Spain*
Japan*	United Kingdom
Mexico*	U.S. Territories: Guam, Puerto Rico

*Countries visited more than one time.

Appendix II

Checklists

These checklists are offered for your review in this appendix as *guides*. They are not arranged in any particular order. Just give them a good look and use them as aids to your preparations. They can be tweaked with additions or deletions according to your needs.

Getting Started/Pre-Trip Preparations Checklist

- Prioritize your list of desired destinations.
- Determine the approximate duration of your journey.
- What will be the focus of your trip (sight-seeing, adventure, animal observation, etc.)?
- Consult your travel agent, travel-experienced friends, and other noncommercial resources.
- Consider additional (commercial) travel services such as Travelocity and Expedia.
- Determine your desired types of accommodations.
- Consider your preferred methods of travel.
- Consider the best use of any frequent flyer miles you may own.

- Be sure to give serious thought to travel companion possibilities. Are you better off traveling alone?
- Do you have special dietary needs? If so, be sure to include this in your planning.
- Consider how you will communicate with friends, family, business associates, etc., and plan accordingly.
- Notify individuals and entities of your travel plans (e.g., credit card companies, banks, mortgage company, landlord, utility companies, and tax preparer).
- Check the expiration date of your passport. Will it expire within six months of your planned return?
- Check the expiration date of your driver's license. Will it expire within thirty days of your planned return?
- Locate your SCUBA certification card if you plan on diving. Get recertified if you haven't gotten wet for over a year.
- Be sure that direct deposit is in place for all sources of income, including salary, pensions, and social security.
- Set up auto-pay for all recurring expenses and payments, such as mortgage, rent, car payments, and insurance premiums, and credit cards.
- Get an ATM card.
- Obtain a credit card that does not charge a fee for international transactions.
- Arrange for home care, pet care, mail, etc.
- Don't forget your health checks. (Please see the next checklist.)
- Are your health insurance and life insurance policies adequate and in order?
- Be sure to seriously consider purchasing travel insurance.

- Give a heads-up to friends and family members who live in places on your itinerary.
- Be sure that your will and advance health care directive (i.e., living will) are current.
- Make arrangements for filing your income tax if you will be on the road during tax time.

Preliminary Health Checklist
- Doctor(s):

  Physical exam to include:
  - a thorough check-up;
  - a thorough review of meds and supplements needed for trip *and* prescriptions/orders for more as necessary while on the road (Don't forget to consider motion sickness and altitude sickness meds.);
  - a review of needed vaccinations and prophylaxis regimens (e.g., malaria prophylaxis, yellow fever shot and card that proves that you have had a vaccination, Hep B series, tetanus shot, etc.); and
  - a weight and fitness check (Is there a need for dieting and/or a fitness program?).
- Specialists:
  - wellness doctor
  - dermatologist
  - eye doctor
  - chiropractor
- Dentist:
  - a thorough check up
  - a cleaning

        o   address all acute and long-term needs: fillings, crowns, root canals, etc.

Packing Checklist
- Documents
    - o   passport (Check for expiration date, need for extra pages, reciprocity fees, difficult-to-obtain visas, etc.)
    - o   itinerary
    - o   tickets and vouchers
    - o   ample meds and supplements
    - o   prescriptions and doctors' orders
    - o   copies of important vaccination certificates (e.g., yellow fever card)
    - o   health insurance information (e.g., policy number, contact details, claim forms)
    - o   travel insurance information (e.g., policy number, contact details, claim forms)
    - o   copies (certified) of birth certificate and social security card
    - o   driver's license
    - o   SCUBA certification card (if you plan to do any diving)
    - o   extra recent passport-sized photos
    - o   US currency (Amounts will vary according to the duration of the trip, your destinations, etc. Consult with your travel agent.)
    - o   If you have a military ID, leave it at home along with your original birth certificate and social security card.
- Clothing

This list is going to vary a great deal depending on

such factors as length of travel, itinerary, type of traveling, individual taste, etc. My recommendation is "two Cs and a V":

- o casual
- o comfortable
- o versatile

In addition to the obvious things, be sure to bring appropriate footwear, rain gear, hat(s) that give you proper protection from the sun, long-sleeve shirt(s), and pants.

- Medicine and Supplements
  - o sea-sickness pills and altitude sickness meds if needed[34]
  - o other area-related items such as malaria prophylaxis
- Electronic Devices

  Once again, the needs of travelers will differ here. Some items that you may want to consider include mobile phone, laptop/iPad, chargeable camera(s), *compact* hair dryer, charger(s), adaptor(s), etc.

- Miscellaneous
  - o a few especially helpful travel books and brochures
  - o business cards/calling cards
  - o reliable and durable watch
  - o ear plugs
  - o sunglasses (two pairs with polarized lenses)

---

[34] If you are planning mountain activity—anything above eight thousand feet (twenty-five hundred meters), you should consider taking along altitude sickness meds. Make this subject part of your pre-trip medical examination and consultation. But also remember that *best* way to prevent altitude sickness is through proper acclimatization.

- o basic toiletries
- o dental care products
- o small first-aid kit (bandages, antiseptic, antihistamine, analgesic, aspirin, cotton swabs, etc.)
- o tummy tonic (e.g., Pepto or something stronger …)
- o sunscreen (You can always buy this almost anywhere you travel.)
- o insect repellant (with DEET)
- o several pairs of reading glasses if needed
- o small flashlight/torch
- o headlamp
- o pens, pencils, writing tablet(s)
- o walking stick(s), supports, braces as needed
- o a few zip lock bags of various sizes
- o money belt
- o small calculator
- o multi-purpose gloves
- o list of important contacts (kept on Smart Phone, address book, etc.)
- o additional battery and memory cards for camera(s)
- o small bottle of Superglue
- o needle and thread
- o easy-to-pack water bottle

Appendix III

Reading List and Research Resources

AARP publications

Arrivalguides.com

Concierge.com

ENISA Publications and advisories

Fodor's Travel Guides

Frommer's Guides

Lonely Planet Guides

Rough Guides

Ruba (on-line only)

Specialized guides and publications on individual countries, regions, continents, food, culture, adventure, museums, sports, language, etc.

Travel as a Political Act and virtually any other book by Rick Steves

Trip Advisor

Tripwolf

United States Department of State travel information and advisories—hard copy and on-line web site: (travel.state.gov/travel)

Wikitravel

Yahoo Travel

Yellow Book (CDC)

Index

CPSIA information can be obtained at www.ICGtesting.com
Printed in the USA
BVOW07s0040230914

367881BV00001B/20/P